ENDORSEMENTS

As the mother of three girls , two being teenagers I was honored to review this book with my daughters . There is so much information coming at our young girls trying to define what beauty is, and where their value comes from. This book helped them see and focus on Godly truth , and coach them in a way they could relate.

MICHELLE AGUERREVERE

This book is a must-have! Value comes intrinsically from being fearfully and wonderfully made, not by how symmetrical your face is or what you ate for lunch! Being a girl is tough! There are so many fake standards, comparisons, and/or competitions placed on us, which is why this book is so powerful! It reorients and renews the mind away from the drudgery of believing you have to go viral on TikTok or get compliments on social media from strangers. Instead, the book walks through practical steps to fully grow into your potential and power.

Grace Field
Broadway Actress
(Disney on Broadway, Hercules)

I appreciate the educational perspective of the experienced young women breathing into the insecurities and curiosities of younger girls. In our post-feminist culture, it's important to reaffirm their honest, feminine convictions and value in the sight of God.

Sam Sorbo
Filmmaker and
Education Freedom Advocate

If you need some help with trying to figure out this crazy world - especially the unrealistic social media world versus reality as a teen girl - then this guide is for you. One of my favorite messages was about living in the moment in every way and being kind to yourself as you would to others.

Livi Birch
Actress
(Alice Creel in Stranger Things,
Young Belle in The Farmer and The Belle)

As someone who spends hours with teens and young adults through Christian camping, I know the issues young women face today. This book touches on all the topics close to a teen's heart. It is well organized with stories teens can relate to, prayers to bring one closer to God, call-outs to affirm who you are, and questions for deeper thinking. This is a book for every teen girl. It will help them understand who they are and bring them closer to God.

Chrys Howard
Bestselling Author and Speaker,
Director at Camp Ch-Yo-Ca,
grandmother of Sadie Robertson

A must-read for every young girl or woman to know that they are so much more than likes and society's beauty standard.

Hailey Julia
Social Media Influencer,
TikTok @HaileyJulia_, IG: @HaileyJulia_

Being a young woman is hard, to say the least. The enemy is constantly using television, movies, and social media to redefine the definition of beauty, and the impact is devastating. Everywhere you look, you see a "perfect image" that becomes the standard by which beauty is measured. The problem is that the perfect image has been filtered, and it's so far from God's definition of true beauty. Jenn and her team remind us that we can break the cycle and experience true freedom. When we see ourselves through the eyes of Jesus, we discover the confidence that we are His masterpiece.

Shannen Fields
Award-Winning Actress
(Facing the Giants, The Order of
Rights), Producer, Writer, and
Inspirational Speaker

As a teenage girl with a physical disability, sometimes my appearance is what I use to measure my worth. I love learning that it doesn't matter what other people think about my inner and outer beauty but how God views me. I recommend this devotional to all teen girls. The lessons it teaches are impeccable. It covers the ideas of identity, worth, and physical appearance.

Grace Nova
Social Media Influencer & Musician
@TheGraceNova

Beauty & Likes from The Farmer and The Belle is a reminder that no matter what you are going through, you can prevail, and there's always hope.

Whitney Reynolds
Host & Executive Producer,
Whitney Reynolds Show

Beauty & Likes

© 2022 by The Farmer and The Belle Publishing.

Published by The Farmer and The Belle Publishing.
P.O Box 929 West New York, NJ 07093
(917) 818-4792. thefarmerandthebelle.usa@gmail.com

Design by Madeline King | maddiemaestudios.com
Editorial services by Dr. Lynnette Simm | Drlms96@gmail.com
Printed in Korea

ISBN: 978-1-7334694-4-9 (Paperback)

21 22 23 24 25 26 27 7 6 5 4 3 2 1

THE AMAZON BEST SELLING MOVIE, "THE FARMER AND THE BELLE,"
BRINGS YOU THE DIVINE BEAUTY COLLECTION.

BEAUTY & LIKES

EXPERIENCING GOD'S TRUTH
ABOUT YOUR LOOKS

MORGAN THREADGILL & JENN GOTZON
WITH DR. LYNNETTE SIMM

HI CHICKAS!

You are being prayed for as you read this. Every paragraph has a new surprise in it for you to discover. Our team of teenage and young adult writers and contributors worked hard to craft each word to bring you hope and a new understanding of beauty.

My name is Jenn Gotzon. I'm an actress who started my journey at the age of 15 in a small town surrounded by cornfields in Pennsylvania. Growing up, I struggled with acne and desperately wanted to be liked by those around me. I strived for perfection. We didn't have social media back then. When I was your age, the computer was just coming out. Seriously! I'm still a hot mess on IG trying to figure out stories. LOL (and true!). So, I formed a team of young adults to write this book specifically for you. Get to know them on pages 139-141. Each chapter's direction came from the research I did for our movie, The Farmer and The Belle: Saving Santaland.

My mama bear, Jo-Ann Gotzon, and my Pop-Pop (her dad) showed me the power of prayer.

Lemme pray for you now:
"Dear Jesus, walk hand-in-hand with our beautiful friend holding this book right now. Give her the courage to look into the mirror of her soul. Open her heart to see you, Jesus, looking back at her in the reflection. Help her transform her mind with your truth found in the Bible. Let her relate to Morgan's stories and the therapeutic insight from Dr. Simm. Let the prayers speak refreshment over her body. Give her the determination to go deep with the questions, finding the root of the negative lies spoken over her. Help her to find freedom in Your love. We pray this in your holy name, Jesus. Amen."

Sending you my deepest love.
Keep in touch on IG and FB @JennGotzon.

Warmest blessings,

Jenn Gotzon

FORWARD
SCHOLARSHIP OPPORTUNITY

Fanchon Stinger

Television host, Co-founder & CEO Grit & Grace Nation, Speaker

It's a vivid metaphor for how to live out grit and grace. The majestic animal athletes are bred to naturally buck. I own two beautiful bucking bulls, Stinger and Lil Hott, who are loved like family. The bull's job? Buck off the bull rider. The rider's job? Ride for 8 secs. It's the toughest 8 secs in sports, just like life can sometimes be. When the professional bull riders get bucked off and banged up, they get back up, fight through the pain and ride again. That's how we develop grit and grace in life. We hold on to faith with a grip like a bull rider.

Grit & Grace Nation and the Professional Bull Riders league (PBR) alliance is exceptional. Scholarship applicants can get VIP access to America's fastest-growing family-friendly sport.

Apply for a Grit & Grace Leadership Scholarship: www.gritandgracenation.org | @GritAndGraceNation.

God produces grace. We never quit and never lose hope. Girl Grit is the secret to growing the seeds of greatness already within you. You were born to lead with COURAGE, GRIT, AND GRACE! (Jer 29:11, Romans 5: 3-5, Phil 2 3-4).

Grit & Grace Nation: Equipping young ladies through mentorship and scholarships to lead with courage and excellence in ALL they do while honoring Faith, Family, and Freedom.

MORE THAN LIKES

Hailey Julia

Social Media Influencer

TikTok: @HaileyJulia_ IG: @HaileyJulia_

I love social media and the fact that I can use my platform to uplift people and share the love of Jesus, but I also hate it sometimes because of the comparison and insecurity it brings. I used to think that if I just reached ten thousand followers, I'll be happy; if I just got over one thousand likes, I'll be pretty. This is a dangerous cycle of thinking that will leave you disappointed, sad, and alone because the truth is, after reaching those "happiness" goals and surpassing them by a long shot, I still didn't feel happier or prettier. In fact, I felt the opposite.

Comparison started to creep in, and I began to think things like, "wow, I'm actually not that pretty," or "wow, this video didn't get many views or likes; I must not really be funny!" (my content revolves around comedy).

I made the mistake of finding my identity in followers, likes, and views, which brought temporary happiness but left me with a deeper kind of sadness. Once I realized that all of this stuff doesn't matter and that glorifying Jesus is what truly matters, my perspective about myself started to shift. I began to compare myself less and less and love who God created me to be more and more.

Jeremiah 1:5 says, "Before I formed you in the womb, I knew you, before you were born, I set you apart." Social media can be a fantastic tool once you know who God says you are.

A SOUL UNDER CONSTRUCTION

Michelle Daigle

By Kendall Daigle's mother, Michelle, in her remembrance.
Mom/Outreach Coordinator for Kendall Cares

Kendall was a soul that spent nineteen years on this planet before passing away from an unintentional drug overdose.

She was my child. There are so many tragic things about the loss of Kendall in this world, but the one thing that stands out is that she always wanted to change the world through her having suffered. To assist her in making a difference in the world, I want to introduce everyone to this remarkable young woman.

Kendall stood up for the underdog and tried to connect with the students in the class who were the targets of jokes. Kendall wished for everyone to understand that being unique is not just acceptable but great. This passage from "A Soul Under Construction" shows Kendall reflecting on dealing with recovery and the decline that caused her addiction.

Yes, this thing is with me for the long run. A lot depends upon my decision to succumb or believe in redemption. True, I'm not far along in the destruction of my life, but this is just my beginning. I could turn things around and be successful and fulfilled in my endeavors. That is what my soul wants. But my addict wants to lie on a couch of delusion, aroused by my filthy sense of tranquil apathy.

Be beautiful in your soul, and the beauty will illuminate. Know that your darkest hours give way to illumination. Be fearless in your individuality.

RESET MAKEUP TIPS

Jacqui Phillips
Celebrity Make Up Artist

Being a makeup artist is about making someone look beautiful, more importantly, feel beautiful.

You have seen my work; you just didn't know it.

The three most essential features of applying makeup to create a stunning natural look are the eyes which are the windows to the soul. The lips are the gateway to the world we develop with our words, and the cheeks are an extension of the beauty of fresh, glowing skin.

Mascara should be applied patiently with soft strokes and deliberately to accentuate the eyes. Remember, makeup is an accessory we can use to enhance our outer beauty.

When you "Believe Love Of Ourselves Matters, you B-L-O-O-M into Beautiful!" It's important to remember that your inner beauty radiates inside and out, and there is nothing more beautiful than that. God made you unique, so share your beauty with the world through your loving eyes, kind words, and cheeks that radiate with joy.

You can learn more in Jacqui Phillips's best-selling book RESET: 6 Essential RESETS to a Healthier, Happier You. http://jacquiphillips.tv/

BEAUTY & LIKES

EXPERIENCING GOD'S TRUTH ABOUT YOUR LOOKS

TABLE OF CONTENTS

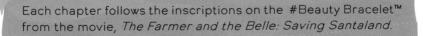

Each chapter follows the inscriptions on the #Beauty Bracelet™ from the movie, *The Farmer and the Belle: Saving Santaland.*

I AM A
MAGNIFICENT
MASTERPIECE

"Body and soul, I am marvelously made!"
Psalm 139:14

I am VALUABLE.
I am MAGNIFICENT.
I am a MASTERPIECE.
I am BEAUTIFUL.
I am MADE BY GOD.

The Lord looks at my heart.
Body and soul,
I am marvelously made.

chapter 1
VALUABLE

WHAT GOD IS SAYING ABOUT YOU:

Just as I considered your life valuable today, so may the Lord consider my life valuable and rescue me from all trouble.
1 Samuel 26:24

BREAKING IT DOWN:

\ 'val-yə-bəl :
possessing traits or qualities that are admired or appreciated.

Being a twenty-something girl in today's world has taught me a lot. I find myself constantly thinking, "I wish I could tell my younger self this or that." Unfortunately, I can't rewind time to tell myself what I have learned, but I can tell others some of my story to help them. For example, I wish I had learned earlier the idea of value.

It is quite easy to make the mistake of measuring your worth as we measure so much of our lives. Sadly, we might use the number of 'likes' we get on social media, our score in whatever competition we are in, our grades, or our clothes size to measure our value. Humans love to assign value to things so we can comprehend their worth.

You are valuable in God's eyes no matter what.

I like using Instagram. I love the feed I have developed, and I love seeing what people are up to. However, social media can create a mindset of negative feelings towards ourselves and others by constantly comparing ourselves to people we do and do not know. I know the feeling when you're scrolling and seeing a girl the same age who seems to have perfect skin, body, or life. I can't even tell you how many times I have posted a picture that I liked, just to delete it an hour later because I didn't get the likes I wanted. I get it.

I am sitting here, as a twenty-four-year-old, struggling with the same concept you are, my value. I often feel empty because I have placed my value in validation from crushes, social media, friends, clothes, grades, etc. I didn't realize I put my value in these things until about a year ago when I was talking to this boy. I really

16

liked him, and we talked every day for about 4 months. One day, I got a text that I wasn't expecting, basically saying, while he had fun, he didn't want a relationship with me. But all my brain comprehended was he didn't want me. I wasn't worth it. He walked away, and with him went my value. "He didn't pick me — I am worthless," were the most untrue words I have ever said to myself.

EXPERIENCE YOUR BEAUTY

Did you know that positive self-talk, also known as affirmations, can alter your brain and change your mood? Repeating out loud positive phrases can give them power because we tend to believe what we hear. So, try saying these true phrases to yourself in a mirror... I am extraordinary. I am worthy. I am valuable.

Isaiah 43:4 states, "you are precious in my eyes and honored, and I love you." When you learn to change your "self-talk" from negative to positive and learn to look from the outside to inside, the faster your life will change. Jesus only says positive things about you, and He sees all of you, inside and out. You are important and worthy!

LET'S TALK TO GOD

Dear Lord, examine my heart and help me see myself as valuable as you created me. Help me identify why I don't feel valuable and sew up my wounds with your unconditional love giving me the strength to forgive those negative words and memories holding me hostage. Please bring me the freedom to experience my value in you, Jesus. Amen!

REPEAT IN YOUR MIND & SHINE!

Say over yourself 30x today:

"I AM valuable."

TAKE ACTION

1. Where do you currently find your value? What steps can you take to stop letting others assign value to you?

2. When was the last time you felt truly valuable?

3. Have you ever thought of your value on a sliding scale (today, I am valuable because my crush liked my picture, yesterday, I wasn't valuable because I got a C on my test)? Why or why not?

_____

_____

_____

_____

_____

_____

How does it affect the mirror of your heart to know that God says you are valuable?

chapter 2

MAGNIFICIENT

WHAT GOD IS SAYING ABOUT YOU:

The princess looks absolutely magnificent, decked out in pearls and clothed in a brocade trimmed with gold.
Psalm 45:13

BREAKING IT DOWN:

\ mag-'ni-fə-sənt :
awe-inspiring in the mind or spirit.

I was talking to one of my best friends, and she asked a question that startled me. "Do you believe in God?" I thought to myself, "Shouldn't the answer be obvious?" I replied, "Yes." We continued talking and moved on to characteristics we have witnessed in some people of God. We both described a captivating feature about them, a radiating fire within them that emulates a positive energy. My friend knew exactly what I was talking about. It's this indescribable characteristic that comes from within for all to see. We started listing off people we knew in high school who had this quality, and landed on a girl named Claire.

> Let God in and trust him.
> This makes your heart magnificent.

Claire was a down-to-earth person who was always smiling. She wasn't particularly popular, but everyone knew who she was. Everyone would describe her as kind, welcoming, happy, and a God-like person. By just looking at Claire, you could tell there was something captivating about her. You wanted merely to be near her because she had a notable and magnificent energy.

One day Claire sat down next to me at lunch; I asked why she seemed happy all the time. She replied, "I'm not happy all the time. I am just trusting." When she saw I was confused, she continued, "I trust God has a plan for me. I am not worried. I give all my worries to Him. I trust Him, and His love for me. Somedays are hard to trust, and I want to take control, but then I return to Him who knows what's best for me. He knows my heart and what I need versus what I think I want."

20

People wanted to be near Claire because she radiated Jesus, who lives inside her. She has a magnificent soul in her walk with Christ, not merely a beautiful vessel. The captivating light is not how you look; it's who you are as a person and how you share what captives you.

I realized I needed to put my trust in God's plan for me. It's not easy, but every night when I pray, I ask God to light a fire inside me. I ask Him to lead the way and help me follow the path He has set for me, even if I don't understand the plan. I ask Him to use me to help others and give me opportunities to share about Him.

EXPERIENCE YOUR BEAUTY

Psychologists describe your notable personality as what makes you who you are and influences everything from your relationships to how you live. Once you realize how important you are to our Heavenly Father, characteristics such as integrity, patience, and steadfastness will show you that you have a divine purpose in this world that no one else can do except for you. These characteristics aren't found in your outer beauty, talents, skills, or your grades. They are found in how you treat others and yourself.

TODAY'S PRAYER

Dear Lord, I speak to my soul wounds and the pain within my heart that makes me believe I am nothing. I rebuke those thoughts in the name of Jesus and hold them captive, giving each one of those memories into the hand of Jesus. Please open my eyes to wash with your truth that I am MAGNIFICENT! Because you created me! Please, Jesus, help me believe this. In your name, amen.

21

REPEAT IN YOUR MIND & SHINE!
Say over yourself 30x today:

"I AM magnificent."

TAKE ACTION

1. What are some traits that make your soul magnificent?

2. Are you surrounding yourself with people who have a fire within them?

3. Who in your life needs to be reminded that God created them in his own image, and he doesn't make mistakes? Is that person you?

_____

_____

_____

_____

_____

_____

_____

How does it affect the mirror of your heart to know that you can become magnificent for God?

chapter 3

MASTERPIECE

WHAT GOD IS SAYING ABOUT YOU:

For we are God's masterpiece. He
has created us anew in Christ Jesus,
so we can do the good things he
planned for us long ago.
Ephesians 2:10

BREAKING IT DOWN:

\ 'ma-stər-,pēs :
a task completed with exceptional
expertise in particular: the pinnacle
of human knowledge or creativity.

My body is covered in bruises, welts, bumps, and many irritation marks. You see, I have type one diabetes. My body doesn't make insulin to regulate my blood sugar. So, I have the lovely job of manually giving myself a shot of insulin every time I eat. I also have acne, wrinkles, stretch marks, and cellulite. I am not perfect, not even in the slightest, so the word masterpiece is not exactly how I would describe myself.

When I think of a masterpiece, my brain thinks of art. You know, Van Gogh, Picasso, Monet, and others. These artists' paintings aren't necessarily beautiful, but they are masterpieces, each in their own way. Each painting, sculpture, or drawing has a purpose. Each piece is exceptional for telling a story, capturing a moment, or simply explaining how something was done. God gave these artists a purpose, and they carried it out in their work. They created what the world considers to be masterpieces. God's masterpieces are when He created them and you.

To God, you are a beautiful masterpiece, His masterpiece. You are constantly changing and evolving in His creation. Being a masterpiece may not resemble what you think you look like, but you are a masterpiece because you are God's greatest work. In Genesis, when He is creating the land, the sky, and the animals, God says, "and that is good." When he created man, He said, "and that is very good."

You are God's greatest masterpiece!

A masterpiece is said to be one of a kind, which is crazy because so are you. "I praise You, for I am awesomely,

24

wonderfully made! Marvelous are Your works; and my soul knows that right well" (Psalms 139:14). That's right, YOU were perfectly made. Each and every part of you was created with a purpose.

Some might say my body is broken, BUT GOD says I am perfectly and wonderfully made. I can't begin to tell you how God has used my diabetes for His plans. For example, I met my best friends through being diabetic. I have spoken in front of thousands of people about having diabetes. I have helped many parents with kids who have type one diabetes. And I know He is not done with me yet.

EXPERIENCE YOUR BEAUTY

How we see our own bodies is important. We are not too tall, short, thin, or big. We are not broken because we have medical, educational, mental, or physical differences. How we view ourselves can cause great joy or deep disappointment. Choose JOY. Our bodies and minds are always changing, especially during adolescence, so it's vital for us to be kind to ourselves. We need to treat ourselves and our bodies just as we would treat our best friends. Love where and who you are right now because you will not be that person tomorrow.

TODAY'S PRAYER

Dear Lord, I am your masterpiece. Why don't I believe this? My tears fill my eyes. I don't understand how to create this truth inside my soul, but you can. Speak to my innermost parts and tell me that I am your beloved masterpiece. Help me see myself as radiant as the most magnificent sunset, a masterpiece of your creation. In your name Jesus, Amen.

TAKE ACTION

1. Why is it often so difficult to believe that you are God's masterpiece?

2. What are some of your marks that make you a masterpiece?

3. Masterpieces are often around for centuries. What do you hope to leave behind someday?

_____

_____

_____

_____

_____

_____

_____

How does it affect the mirror of your heart to know that God says you are a masterpiece?

chapter 4
BEAUTIFUL

WHAT GOD IS SAYING ABOUT YOU:

How beautiful you are, my darling.
How very beautiful!
Your eyes are doves.
Song of Solomon 1:15

BREAKING IT DOWN:

\ 'byü-ti-fəl :
having attractive qualities:
generating aesthetic delight.
generally positive.

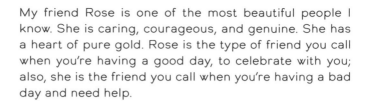

My friend Rose is one of the most beautiful people I know. She is caring, courageous, and genuine. She has a heart of pure gold. Rose is the type of friend you call when you're having a good day, to celebrate with you; also, she is the friend you call when you're having a bad day and need help.

Rose has an exceptional work ethic. She starts work at 6 am and won't stop until 6 pm, on most days. Rose takes work seriously. As my roommate and friend, I texted her that I was having a bad day with a lot of anxiety. Two minutes later, Rose walked through my door and said, "What are we doing?" I was confused until she added, "Get up. We're going on a walk." This small gesture was meaningful to me. Rose put me first without hesitation. She helped me get out of my own head. Her heart is the most beautiful part of her.

True beauty starts from within yourself.

It is true; beauty comes from within. For generations, beauty has been based on outer appearance. But what if it wasn't? What if we didn't look down on ourselves for not meeting others' beauty expectations? What if we didn't edit our photos on social media? Too many girls and guys struggle to see their outer beauty because they constantly compare themselves to others. We must remember that physical beauty standards change often.

The Bible mentions outer beauty; however, it also states that physical beauty should be secondary to character. I want women to adorn themselves with proper clothing, modestly, and discreetly, not with braided hair and gold or pearls or costly garments, but rather by means of

28

good works, as is proper for women making a claim of godliness."
1 Timothy 2:9-10

EXPERIENCE YOUR BEAUTY

Do you love your friends for how they look or for who they are? The answer is probably like Morgan, she loves Rose for her kindness and caring. Would Rose's kindness have been less beautiful if her hair was in a messy bun? Nope. Researchers have found that the most beautiful people are those who have beautiful qualities, positive attitudes, and share those characteristics with others.

Outer beauty is subjective, meaning everyone will like different things. For example, what is your favorite color, beach or mountains, impressionist art or photographs? See there are so many opinions when it comes to outer beauty. But inner beauty can be seen by everyone, like grace, kindness, gentleness, and honesty. Also, outer beauty might be altered, for example different clothes or hairstyles, but inner beauty will last. Friendly, joyful, thoughtfulness, patient, forgiving, courage, humble, and loving are all beautiful parts of a person that will grow more and more beautiful each day.

TODAY'S PRAYER

Dear Jesus, Do you really believe that I am beautiful? How can you when I see all my flaws in the mirror, my weight, my looks, my hair? Help me right now to close down those negative thoughts and open my eyes, transform how I see myself and let me see beauty in all my features. Right now, in the name of Jesus, I BELIEVE I am beautiful. I stand on this truth today and forever in Jesus' name. Amen!

REPEAT IN YOUR MIND & SHINE!

Say over yourself 30x today:

"I AM beautiful."

TAKE ACTION

1. How can being vain affect you and your relationships?

2. When you take away the adornments, who are you?

3. What are words you use to describe your friends? Did you describe them with just physical descriptors, or did you describe who they are as a person?

_____

_____

_____

_____

_____

_____

_____

How does it affect the mirror of your heart to know that God says you are beautiful?

chapter 5

MADE BY GOD

WHAT GOD IS SAYING ABOUT YOU:

So God created man in His own image, in the image and likeness of God He created him; male and female He created them.
Genesis 1:27

BREAKING IT DOWN:

\ 'mād \ 'bī \ 'gäd :
made of numerous components, revered as the universe's creator and ruler and perfect in power, wisdom, and goodness.

Have you ever heard that your thoughts become your reality?

Imagine you are standing in front of a mirror. If I asked you to get the reflection to wave, you would simply wave. If I said to make the reflection wink, you would wink. Now, if you take the mirror away and put a person in front of you, the dynamic doesn't change. If I said to get the person to wave, you would simply wave first. Let's take this one step further and say I want this person to laugh. While you could try and do something funny or make a joke, you are actually making yourself laugh first with something you think is funny. The last one... try and make the person in front of you love you, what would you have to do? Loving them is nice and might work, but the answer is you have to love yourself first.

God made you for a reason.

To get something from someone else, you must give it to yourself first. How do you expect someone to give you something if you don't have it or don't believe in it? Life is a reflection of ourselves.

Loving who I am is something I still struggle with. The pressing questions of: Is this cool? Will people make fun of me?, and Am I good enough? Enter my head more often than I would like to admit. I still must remind myself that it doesn't matter. God made me, me. He gave me unique quirks, passions, and talents. So, it doesn't matter if what makes me happy doesn't make sense to someone else; it doesn't have to. That's part of what makes life so fun; we're all different.

EXPERIENCE YOUR BEAUTY

Isaiah 64:8 says, "O Lord, You are our Father, we are the clay, and You our potter; and all of us are the work of Your hand." You are enough, exactly as you are. God molded you and formed you into exactly who you are supposed to be. And He will keep molding you as time goes on. All the things that make you different are enough because God said they are.

Did you know relationship researchers say that "The person who smiles all the time offers unconditional love to those dear to them?" That person is reflecting the loving relationship they have with themselves and have learned to love their innermost being. That innermost being is the one God created. The best way to love your innermost being is to acknowledge all the amazing things that make you different, special, and unique. Try making a list of all your God-given attributes – intellectually, emotionally, and physically. I, Dr. Lynnette, love my ability to learn sign language. I love my kindness to my cousins. I love my ears. Keep going... what do you love about YOU?

TODAY'S PRAYER

My Father in Heaven, I praise you, for you are glorious and praise-worthy. Breath upon me so I can feel and believe you made me. That you truly made me. Let me see myself in the mirror, and on the posts I make as you see me: beautiful and fearfully made by you. In your name Jesus, Amen.

TAKE ACTION

1. What are some of your unique qualities that make you, you?

2. Why do we care so much about what other people will think of us?

3. Does knowing that you are good enough for The King of Kings ease the pressure of what others think?

_____

_____

_____

_____

_____

_____

_____

How does it affect the mirror of your heart to know that you are made by God?

chapter 6

LOOK AT MY HEART

WHAT GOD IS SAYING ABOUT YOU:

For the Lord sees not as man sees;
for man looks at the outward
appearance, but the Lord looks
at the heart.
1 Samuel 16:7

BREAKING IT DOWN:

\ ˈlu̇k \ at \ ˈmī \ ˈhärt :
to determine by the use of one's eyes
the intention behind a presumed
action that pertains to my personality,
disposition, or ethic.

The other day I realized I am chasing an image. I often catch myself looking into a mirror, wondering if I'd be more desirable if I was thinner, taller, shorter, straight, or curly hair, tanned, or pale. I mentally list everything I want to change about myself rather than concentrating on what I like about myself. I, too often, tell myself I need to have this person's face, hair, or body to be accepted or loved. I'm chasing an image that the world, media, and social media tell me I need to be.

Stop comparing your outer image because God only cares for your heart.

When we look into a mirror, our brains quickly recognize the face in the mirror as ours. God gave us this learned skill even though over time our faces continuously change, from birth till now, yet our brains learn to see ourselves. Remarkable. Yet, we diminish ourselves by comparing. Comparison increases self-loathing and steals our joy. Stop looking at others and take a deeper look at that beautiful face looking back at you.

I will never see myself as others see me. I won't see my eyes light up when I talk about something I am passionate about. I don't notice how I dance when I eat something I like. I don't experience my smile when my friends make me laugh. All I can see is a moment captured through a lens, a reflection staring back, or a single image sitting there. I assume the person staring back at me isn't good enough. I need to be something more.

I challenged myself. Without any context, I asked my family and friends to describe me as if they were talking to someone else. Here is what I got: witty, smart, kind, generous, strong, pretty (thanks, mom), loyal, a good friend, someone who is level headed, a role model, a girlboss, independent, and so on. Now, you ask your family and friends. You might be pleasantly surprised.

EXPERIENCE YOUR BEAUTY

Another way to see your extraordinary self is to stay away from social media. Why? Because all those 'likes' and 'hearts' are comparison traps. You're comparing yourself to another person's highlight reel. As one teen editor said, "Quite often, social media includes the highlights of a person's life exclusively, but they experience struggles and insecurities just like us, so we must not fall to comparison."

Comparisons keep you focused on what you are not versus what God made you to be. When God looks at you, He sees you as a person, not what you look like as a person. The scar you might hate, He sees a story that adds to you. The legs you wish were skinnier, He sees the strength you have to carry you. Human bodies are made to grow, shrink, and change throughout life. Celebrate it because God thinks you're perfect, just the way you are.

TODAY'S PRAYER

Wow, Lord... look at my heart and cleanse me with your unconditional love. Help me hold captive those nasty things people have snared over me with their comments or looks. Forgive my heart for being defeated and not coming to you for my love and acceptance. Heal my heart and allow me to shine for you today and always, Jesus. Smile through me. In your name, Lord, Amen.

REPEAT IN YOUR MIND & SHINE!
Say over yourself 30x today:

"THE LORD looks at the heart."

TAKE ACTION

1. What are the stories your body tells about God's plan for you?

2. What will God find when he searches your heart?

3. Are you chasing an image? What are some ways to recognize that and change the narrative?

_____

_____

_____

_____

_____

_____

_____

What does it do to the mirror of your heart to know
that God is searching there?

chapter 7

MARVELOUSLY MADE

WHAT GOD IS SAYING ABOUT YOU:

Body and soul, I am marvelously made! You know me inside and out, you know every bone in my body; You know exactly how I was made, bit by bit.

Psalm 139:14-16

BREAKING IT DOWN:

\ 'märv-(ə-)ləs \ 'mād :
the best possible combination of qualities: of the greatest collection of attributes.

For my mom and I, jeans shopping is the worst. My mom is 5'7" tall, smaller framed, with some curves. I am 5'9" tall, medium build, with a big booty. Finding the perfect pair of denim is tough for us both. Mom prefers nothing too tight, a skinnier leg, mid-rise jeans. I prefer a variety of styles, something that won't look cropped when it isn't supposed to be, and high-rise jeans. We both struggle to find a jean that is comfortable around our thighs, not too tight, and doesn't leave a gap at our waist.
Sound familiar?

After the 3rd attempt of sucking it in to button a pair of jeans, my mom looked at me and said, "Those jeans just aren't made for you, and that's okay." On the verge of tears, because the size I want and normally fit isn't fitting, I asked myself a few questions. One: why am I trying to fit into clothes when clothes are made to fit us? Two: why won't I get a bigger size when no one sees the label inside my pants, anyway? Three: what am I trying to prove with these pants, and who am I trying to prove it to?

Your Body and soul are marvelously made!

Still, as a 24-year-old woman, jean shopping is hard. Jeans need to be a certain size, and we try everything to not go up a size and everything to go down one. Jean fabrics vary. You can find 99% cotton with no stretch—you can barely breathe, 30% elastic—you can do the splits, and everything in between. There are brands that make many versions of their pants with options of rise, wash, distressing, and cuts you want. Don't waste time and your heart trying to fit into something that isn't made for you! There are other options out there perfectly made for you.

EXPERIENCE YOUR BEAUTY

Psychologists coined the term "enclothed cognition" to explain the complicated relationship humans have with clothes. What we wear can influence our mood, behaviors, and thoughts, and what others wear can cause us to stereotype them. Also, psychologists discovered that confidence in clothes is just as important as the material itself. Walking with confidence can show determination and intelligence, and create a great first impression. Own your beauty, your uniqueness, and your clothes.

As one teen editor said, "Confidence is a process that I myself am still trying to achieve, but when I am feeling dejected, I try to remember that no matter the size, color, style, or brand name of the clothes I wear, I am beautifully and wonderfully made." There are girls out there just like you. The struggle is real, but you can be encouraged that you are beautifully and wonderfully made too!

TODAY'S PRAYER

For I am marvelously made. Lord, do I really believe this? If I am truthful, I may question this when I compare myself to another in the classroom, on social media, or at a party or the mall. Help me see myself as you see me. Marvelously made! Majestic is your masterpiece. Precious and the ruby of your eye. Yes, help me see myself in your eyes. I praise you, Lord, Amen.

REPEAT IN YOUR MIND & SHINE!

Say over yourself 30x today:

"I AM marvelously made."

TAKE ACTION

1. What physical things control you, and how are they keeping you from serving Jesus?

2. Why do you try to fit inside something that isn't made for you? What are you trying to prove, and who are you trying to prove it to?

3. What are two ways your soul could soar for God?

_____

_____

_____

_____

_____

_____

How does it affect the mirror of your heart to know that God says both your body and soul are marvelously made?

I AM AN
OVERCOMER

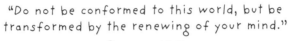

"Do not be conformed to this world, but be
transformed by the renewing of your mind."
Romans 12:2

I am TRANSFORMED.
I am an OVERCOMER.
I am RENEWING MY MIND.

I will bring the lie into the light
and replace it with God's truth.
He heals the brokenhearted.

chapter 8
TRANSFORMED

WHAT GOD IS SAYING ABOUT YOU:

And do not be conformed to this world [superficial customs], but be transformed by the renewing of your mind [focusing on godly values and ethical attitudes] Romans 12:2

BREAKING IT DOWN:

\ tran(t)s-'form :
to alter the external form or appearance of something, its nature, its state, its composition, or its structure.

Social media has tons of makeup, hair, and even weight loss transformation posts. You know, the ones with the dramatic before and after photos. I've never had a dramatic external change to post; however, the other day, my pastor said something that really struck me. He said, "Jesus didn't just resurrect all those years ago, but he is constantly resurrecting things in our life for his purpose." So yeah, I don't have any transformation photos to post, but I do have a transformation story.

Working on yourself helps you transform.

One of the hardest times of my life was when I was diagnosed with a depressive state. I couldn't even say the words out loud because I didn't want to accept it. It's the weirdest feeling: having no motivation, feeling numb, and watching life keep moving, but it feels like you're sitting still. You're battling yourself in your mind— if you just do these things, you'll feel better, but for some reason, you can't do anything.

I had to accept that I did this to myself. I ran my body right into the ground. I wouldn't take a break because I didn't want to deal with what was really wrong. I didn't want to resurrect all my past hurts and heal them, so instead, I avoided and buried them. This avoiding and burying didn't help me at all because my problems were still there. They never disappeared, even when I tried my absolute hardest to ignore them. The weight of my problems only got heavier until it broke me.

With the help and hard work, it took me two long months before I noticed a difference. Have you heard, during the flight safety demonstration, that you must put your own

mask on before you can help others? Every day I woke up and picked myself first, instead of others. I had to learn that I wasn't being selfish by taking care of myself first. I began to notice my transformation and growth. I learned a lot about myself and how I operate. Nothing changed on the outside, but on the inside, I was a new girl.

EXPERIENCE YOUR BEAUTY

Spiritual and emotional/mental changes work that way. You have to do the work for yourself. It might be uncomfortable, confusing, and even aggravating, but that is where the transformation happens, and it is worth it, believe me. No one ever said the transformation was easy, and oftentimes it's not. Seeking help from your parents, trusted adults, professional mentors, counselors, or therapists can help you, but you know who else you can always turn to...Jesus!

Jesus wants to help. He promises to be there for you, always. He works with and in us, transforming our minds and souls. So, spend time with Him in prayer, in worship, talking to Him, and reading His word. The more you do, the greater the transformation you will see in yourself and others will see in you, as well.

TODAY'S PRAYER

Dear Jesus, search my heart right now and my thoughts. Find those silly things I can not stop dwelling on. Appear real to me as if you are sitting next to me right now. Give me the courage to give you those thoughts, so I can believe the truth you tell me in the Bible, in your Word. Strengthen me today to be transformed to be more like you. Kind, loving, and gentle in spirit. Bold and confident like a roaring lion for you. Amen.

REPEAT IN YOUR MIND & SHINE!

Say over yourself 30x today:

"I AM transformed."

TAKE ACTION

1. Why is it important to transform our minds first if we want change to happen?

2. Why is spiritual change sometimes painful?

3. How does transforming our minds tie into becoming inwardly beautiful?

_____

_____

_____

_____

_____

_____

_____

_____

How does it affect the mirror of your heart to know that your heart and life can be transformed?

chapter 9
OVERCOMER

WHAT GOD IS SAYING ABOUT YOU:

I have told you these things, so that in me you may have peace. In this world you will have trouble. But take heart! I have overcome the world.

John 16:33

BREAKING IT DOWN:

\ 'ō-vər-'kə-mər :
a person who is successful in handling or taking control of an issue or situation.

Sometimes, I have a hard time concentrating. My mind can be a jumbled mess of never-ending to-do lists that I start, then I remember something else I am supposed to do, and then start that one. I tend to overthink everything. Sometimes, I play every possible scenario in my head, even simple things like why a person, who I waved to, didn't wave back, but merely smiled. What did I do wrong, are they mad at me, or embarrassed to say hi to me? I can be a perfectionist. Many times, I do a task multiple times until I am satisfied. I might not even share my work because I didn't trust other people to do it right. At times, I would nearly tear myself apart when something isn't what I think is perfect.

> Stop overthinking and overcome your negative thoughts.

Satan is really good at what he does, and he will do everything he can to make you believe you're not worthy. He will try to put thoughts in your mind to convince you that you're not worthy of love...unless you have the highest grade in the class, unless you complete tasks without struggling, or unless you win every time in sports or any competitive event. I used to think, no one else does this. Why am I like this? Why can't I be like my friends who don't struggle like me?

I have learned I am not alone. A teen editor shared, "As young people we often fall into the pit without even realizing we are actively comparing ourselves. I struggle with concentration especially when I have a lot on my plate and I can't seem to focus on one task. That often leads to discouragement and those moments are when you turn to God." I have also learned that comparison is the biggest thief of joy. Cliché? Yes, however, the words hold truth. More often than not we compare ourselves to others even if we don't realize it. Have you ever asked what someone else scored on a test? Ask yourself, why did you ask them that? You're comparing your scores to see who is "better."

EXPERIENCE YOUR BEAUTY

Sadly, we all compare and we look at what we are lacking, instead of what we have. We compare so we can judge our worth and others. We put ourselves on different levels like an ascending staircase, but when God looks down from heaven - all He sees are the tops of our heads, no one greater, higher, or better than another.

Overcoming is realizing that while you may not have every trait, you are exactly the way God wants you to be. One of the coolest things about our God is that He has your back. He promises not to abandon you. He will take all of your fears, anxieties, and struggles off your shoulders because He loves you. You don't have to gain His love with grades, outer beauty, or work. He wants you just the way you are.

TODAY'S PRAYER

Father in heaven, today's message goes deep. Allow me to stop and think about the wisdom you are speaking to my heart. Remind me throughout the day to give my insecurities to you. Help me create in my imagination that you are walking hand in hand with me, holding my hand and whispering to my heart... I love you. Thank you, Jesus. Amen.

TAKE ACTION

1. Why do you so often make comparisons to other people?

2. Who inspires you to be a better Christian? Why?

3. Why is it important for you to become an overcomer?

_____

_____

_____

_____

_____

_____

_____

_____

How does it affect the mirror of your heart to know that you
are an overcomer?

chapter 10
RENEWED

WHAT GOD IS SAYING ABOUT YOU:

Therefore we do not lose heart, but
though our outer man is decaying, yet
our inner man is being renewed
day by day.
2 Corinthians 4:16

BREAKING IT DOWN:

\ ri-'nü :
restore to vitality, perfection, or
make as good as new. to transform
spiritually.

You can most likely find me in all black attire with black winged eyeliner. I tend to eat the same three meals. Going to new places makes me want to curl up in a ball. And re-watching shows is one of my favorite pastimes. I stick to what I know because it's safe. I don't like change; I actually prefer a routine. You see it's hard for me to give up control because I like to know the outcome before it even happens. Change is uncomfortable to me, but a good mentor of mine once told me that change is where growth happens.

Shifting your routine, your way of doing things, or the way you think can alter your life for the better. Not too long ago, I would look in the mirror and tell myself how ugly and unworthy I was. Being in this negative mindset transformed into other areas of my life because I kept telling myself I wasn't good enough. I would seek other people's approval on the outfit I was wearing, the choices I was making, or even the feelings I was feeling.

Work on yourself to transform your mind.

One day my friend Rose heard me say something negative about myself while I was standing in the mirror, and she immediately told me I had to say 3 positive things about myself that weren't surface level (meaning about my looks). As I sat there trying to think, I started to become upset because I couldn't list 3 things I liked about myself, and I knew something needed to change.

One thing I have always liked about myself is that I am one of the most caring people I know, so I started there. As weeks went on, I noticed how much I was complimenting myself, and I started to notice all of the good qualities I possessed. I am strong, independent, faithful, reliable, resilient, motivated, smart, and so much more. The more I told myself these things, the more I believed them.

EXPERIENCE YOUR BEAUTY

A teen editor shared that "renewal breaks my adherence to thought processes that don't line up the truth of Who I am. Those thought processes are comfortable and keep me stuck. Comfortable can be an idol." We need to change our patterns or our thought process to change our outlook on life. But sometimes that is hard.

Another teen editor explains, "I have a lot of negative thoughts due to uncertainty, anxiety, and a dependency on being productive." I, Dr. Lynnette, want you to know that YOU have the ultimate power for renewing your life. A good exercise that can help you is to ask yourself, "what do I like about me, what am I good at?" Take a good look at yourself, like you would a friend, and start making a list of positives things about you. Write them down and post them around your mirror. One small adjustment can make a difference. God made you wonderfully.

TODAY'S PRAYER

Dear Lord, Today, I boldly pray and ask you to help me to know how to renew my mind. Show me the scripture verse that I can believe over myself. Release me from my negative thinking about myself, and let me see myself courageous, fearless, and brilliantly beautiful. Thank you, Jesus, for being my friend and savior. Amen.

REPEAT IN YOUR MIND & SHINE!
Say over yourself 30x today:

"I AM renewed."

TAKE ACTION

1. Why is change, or a time of renewal, sometimes so scary?

2. What are 3 qualities you like about yourself? How can you use those to pursue God?

3. When you step out in faith, why is it important for you to have a Christian friend to walk the journey with you?

_____

_____

_____

_____

_____

_____

_____

How does it affect the mirror of your heart when you go through a time of renewal with God?

chapter 11

REPLACE THE LIE

WHAT GOD IS SAYING ABOUT YOU:

We demolish arguments and every
pretension that sets itself up against
the knowledge of God, and we take
captive every thought to make it
obedient to Christ.
2 Corinthians 10:5

BREAKING IT DOWN:

\ ri-'plās | 'lī :
to go back to the truth from a
maliciously false statement that was
intended to deceive.

I learned this and I want to share some truth with you. Every social media platform is a business; you probably wouldn't be shocked. Their overall goal is to make money. Instagram, Snapchat, TikTok, BeReal, or whatever other social media you're using, are making money from you. These media platforms are free for the user; however, these companies are competing for your time. The more time you spend on their platform, the more money they get. So, these social media companies have done study, after study, after study to get you ADDICTED to their platform.

Snapchat uses streaks and best friends lists. Instagram, intentionally, holds back likes, then notify you all at once to release dopamine. BeReal sends alerts to post then guilts you with FOMO (fear of missing out) on not posting within their time frame. All to get you emotionally connected to their platforms. Social media IS NOT social, and it IS NOT real. When people post only their best or worst, that isn't real life. When these companies manipulate the data or guilt you with alerts, that isn't real. It is all about money, not you.

Don't let social media tear you down!

"The devil targets and isolates the mind." I have never heard a truer statement. And, what better way to do that than with social media companies doing all they can to get you addicted. Addicted to something that screams with each post...you aren't good enough, you don't have this or that, or you will never be like him/her. Addicted to chasing dopamine to provide you with an intense feeling of reward with each like, heart, or swipe.

This type of external validation is how the enemy can work to isolate us. The quicker you realize how the companies are targeting you the easier it will be for you to stop being manipulated by emotions of unworthiness and take the power you have to share love, grace, and understanding on your social media platforms. I was shocked when I learned how being addicted to social media was hurting me. But then, I used my platforms to share God's word, kindness, and help others see their value and inner beauty.

EXPERIENCE YOUR BEAUTY

Good news! You can have social media and God. You can silence your notifications, unfollow people who don't know you, care about you, or want the best for you. You can create a feed of God's love by sharing kindness, truth, and love. God is the truth! He says we are good enough, as He created us. And what we or others post won't change that truth.

God sees our entire life and not just our reel. He knows what we are struggling with behind the screen and loves us, anyways. When we find our validation exclusively on social media, we lose sight of what is important: spreading real love. Love of a person with all their flaws & talents, with all their mistakes & triumphs, and with all their differences & uniqueness.

TODAY'S PRAYER

Jesus, when I look at TikTok, Instagram, Snapchat, and any of the other social media waves... I can not stop comparing myself to the pictures of friends and idols I see. It makes me feel bad inside. Can you transform me to see myself as you see me? A girl with millions of likes, hearts, and kisses from YOU, Jesus. Thank you. I love you, Lord. Thank you.

REPEAT IN YOUR MIND & SHINE!

Say over yourself 30x today:

"I WILL replace the lie with God's truth."

TAKE ACTION

1. Why are we so quick to live through a screen?

2. What lie do you need to forgive and heal from? What truth do you need to believe?

3. In what ways do you recognize Satan targeting you?

How does it affect the mirror of your heart to know that lies will bring you heartache and God's truth will bring you joy?

chapter 12

BROKENHEARTED

WHAT GOD IS SAYING ABOUT YOU:

He heals the brokenhearted And binds up their wounds [healing their pain and comforting their sorrow.]
Psalm 147:3

BREAKING IT DOWN:

\ 'brō-kən-'här-təd :
overpowered by sadness or grief.

My best friend and I talked, every day, for hours on the phone when we were in college. Sometimes we would just sit in silence with each other so we would have each other's company while doing homework or eating dinner. I would see and talk to her every day, even though we were miles apart. Somewhere, somehow, it all seemed to change. So, you can only imagine how hard it was when all of the sudden, one day, we were no longer friends.

God helps put you back together.

You see, I didn't feel like I was being treated right, and after months of expressing my exhaustion and unhappiness to her, I had to simply walk away. I was in what is known as a toxic relationship, which is ANY relationship that makes you feel unsupported, misunderstood, demeaned, or attacked. Basically, I would feel worse rather than better after our time together.

People change. Middle school, high school, college, into adulthood there is a lot of changing and growing. Sometimes people grow apart, but don't realize it. Sometimes people's own hurts start to hurt others. Whatever was happening, I was getting hurt in this relationship.

I wish it could have been a peaceful split; but, words were said that can't be unsaid, multiple people were involved, buried issues surfaced all at once, and deep down I was angry. Angry that it seemed my feelings were not valued. I felt worthless, and angry that I still cared when it felt like she didn't.

This decision to care for myself, create healthy boundaries, and move on from the relationship didn't come easy. It came after a lot of tears, numerous calls to my mom, feeling confused, and asking God for help. I felt broken, and I struggled with losing someone who wasn't actually gone, but our friendship was dead. Grief can sometimes be more painful than the toxic relationship because gone is the dream of life-long friendship and now there is a tainted history with that person, all the while you still feel connected. But this is where God meets you, in the depths of loss and sadness. 2 Corinthians 12:9 says, "My grace is sufficient for you, for my strength is made perfect in weakness."

EXPERIENCE YOUR BEAUTY

God does his best work when life feels chaotic and unsure. During this time of my life, God was doing His work by putting me back together, piece by piece. I learned to lean on Him. It was not a quick process. It was hard to sit in loneliness, pain, and loss until God helped me transform each emotion into peace, gratitude, and love. I was not the same person I was before, but God said, "that's very good." God uses each experience, each relationship, each trial or tragedy to grow our faith, to deepen our love, and to strengthen our souls.

TODAY'S PRAYER

Dear Jesus, when I feel torn down, insulted, and hurt... when I look at my body and flaws in the mirror... I feel sad. Please, Jesus, with your supernatural providential love, blow your favor upon me that I feel your lovelight shine upon me right now and throughout today! Thank you, Jesus. I trust in you.

TAKE ACTION

1. What circumstances have broken your heart and how has that affected you?

2. When do you feel like God does his best work in you?

3. How does God promise to help you in your healing process?

_____

_____

_____

_____

_____

_____

_____

_____

How does it affect the mirror of your heart to know Jesus heals the brokenhearted?

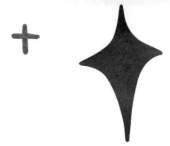

I AM A
JOYFUL GIVER

"Use whatever gift you have received to serve others."

1 Peter 4:10

I am GENEROUS.
I am JOYFUL.
I am A JOYFUL GIVER.

True beauty is serving others.
I use my gifts to serve others.
I am attractive because
I engage in acts of love.

chapter 13
GENEROUS

WHAT GOD IS SAYING ABOUT YOU:

A generous person will prosper;
whoever refreshes others
will be refreshed.
Proverbs 11:25

BREAKING IT DOWN:

\ 'jen-rəs :
generous with gifts.

When I was in high school, there was one kid who was described by everyone as "weird" (we will call him Clark). He was a loner kid who smelled funny and was often the butt of people's jokes. What they didn't know was Clark lived a "Cinderella" life. He was the step-kid of a family that gave everything to his brother. These things included more than just Cinderella's invitation to some fancy ball. I'm talking about how his clothes were hand-me-downs, while his brother's clothes were always new. No hygiene products were bought for him, while his brother was clean cut. And he never got gifts for any occasion, while his brother was showered with gifts.

Generosity can go a long way.

YoungLife, a Christian based organization, was something my family was heavily involved in. They had a "club" which was held every Monday evening at our house, and my brother and I were both involved. One of the leaders was telling my dad about this kid and how he was struggling but that he had a passion for music. Christmas was coming up, and my dad started planning.

My dad went out and bought a basic guitar. He gave it to the YoungLife leader to give to Clark for Christmas. My dad wanted no credit for this gift and told the leader to not let Clark know who bought the guitar. One night after club, Clark was gifted with his guitar. He cried. Clark said that he had never given anything new to call his own. The leader told him that YoungLife got him the guitar.

When my dad told me this story years later, I smiled because generosity can come from anyone. My Dad did something nice for someone, who others looked over. But, the coolest part of the story was that I remembered Clark carrying that guitar around everywhere he went. He played it at pep rallies. He practiced in every corner of the high school. And, he smiled more, a lot more. When I asked my dad why he did this for Clark, he replied with 4 simple words: God told me to.

EXPERIENCE YOUR BEAUTY

Dr. Lynnette's fun facts: Generosity is not only good for the receiver, but for the giver too. Generosity enhances yourself worth, gives life purpose, and helps physically to reduce stress and depression! Giving activates contentment in the brain and stimulates a reward cycle, so the more you give the more your mind, body, and soul enjoys. And, generosity is a natural confidence booster and natural repellent of low self-esteem. Giving helps create strong friendships, happier people, and more satisfaction with who you are!

Who would have thought that being selfless could be so rewarding? God did! He wants us to give to one another, to be generous with our time, talents, and treasures. Give it a try...you may find out that you love giving.

TODAY'S PRAYER

Wow, Lord. I never thought about being generous as a tool of being beautiful. This is a new thought for me. Can you show me where I can be generous? In your name, right now, help me see one of the talents you gave me. Thank you. Now, show me how I can be generous with that gifting. Thank you, Jesus, for showing me this new understanding of beauty.

REPEAT IN YOUR MIND & SHINE!

Say over yourself 30x today:

"I AM generous."

TAKE ACTION

1. Has God ever laid on your heart to give something, and you didn't receive credit for it? How did that make you feel?

2. When is the last time you gave for the sake of giving, instead of for the recognition or benefits that come with it?

3. How can a generous spirit make you a beautiful woman of God?

_____

_____

_____

_____

_____

_____

_____

What does the mirror of your heart reflect about having a generous spirit?

chapter 14

JOYFUL

WHAT GOD IS SAYING ABOUT YOU:

A happy heart makes the face
cheerful, but heartache
crushes the spirit.
Proverbs 15:13

BREAKING IT DOWN:

\ ˈjoi-fəl
experiencing, causing, or displaying
happiness, contentment,
or thankfulness.

Brittany was the bubbliest girl. Her laugh was infectious, her smile lit up the room, and her personality was captivating. It wasn't her make-up that made her beautiful, it was her inner joy that everyone saw on her face.

Unfortunately, my best friend has been through a lot. When she was 23, her little brother died in a car accident. Bryson was only 19. The two had their issues with each other, just like most siblings do. Sadly, their relationship wasn't in the best place when he passed. After Bryson's death, she was so angry, lost, and struggling. Brittany just wasn't herself anymore, and it was written all over her face. Brittany was heartbroken, and no amount of make-up could hide it.

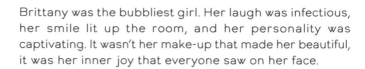

Developing good traits can change your outlook of outer beauty.

I have heard many times, God works in mysterious ways, and His timing is always perfect. It took nearly 2 years before I saw it - Brittany becoming herself again. I heard it from my room...she laughed, a real laugh. I saw the joy all over her face. She looked beautiful at that moment. She had no makeup on, her hair was in a messy bun, she was in sweatpants, yet she was gorgeous. Her smile lit up the entire room, again. While the loss of her brother will stay with her forever, her inner joy did come back with time, and joy is the best make-up!

Proverbs 27:19 says, "As water reflects the face, so a person's heart reflects the person." Anger, sadness, disconnect, grief, peace, joy, and love can all be seen on your face. Sometimes we can spend so much money and time trying to make our outsides look good that we forget that our faces show the world how we are on the inside. If our faces tell our true feelings, then how can we beautify ourselves from the inside out?

EXPERIENCE YOUR BEAUTY

By enhancing your inner beauty first, along with your outer beauty. Negative emotions might hold you back from becoming the person you really want to be, which is why it is so important to give yourself the space and grace to feel those emotions. Sometimes simple things like reading the Bible, devotionals, journaling, music, talking with friends, or just taking a walk can really help release those pent-up emotions. Once you've released the negative emotions then you can see yourself, once again, as the beautiful creation that God made, and the people around you will certainly notice a change in you.

Gentleness, generosity, and honesty are just three inner beauty characteristics. Developing these traits can transform your outer self in to a beauty that shines like a diamond. So how do you get these traits? Ask Jesus. He will guide you through life experiences where you can strengthen each beautiful quality in you.

TODAY'S PRAYER

Jesus, hi, it's me again. How are you? I am well, though I am coming to you again asking for you to show me the mirror how you see me. Show me the unique gifts you have given me. Bring boldness into my soul to use those gifts to serve others today. Help me do this at least one time today. I trust you Jesus for being with me on this. Amen.

REPEAT IN YOUR MIND & SHINE!

Say over yourself 30x today:

"I AM joyful."

TAKE ACTION

1. Why do you spend so much time focusing on your outer appearance and so little time focusing on the inward attributes that will make you truly beautiful?

2. How can joy be one of the best cosmetics?

3. What are two things you can do to share God's joy with someone who needs to experience it?

_____

_____

_____

_____

_____

_____

_____

_____

What does the mirror of your heart reflect about joy?

chapter 15

JOYFUL GIVER

WHAT GOD IS SAYING ABOUT YOU:

Each one of you has received a special gift [a spiritual talent, an ability graciously given by God], employ it in serving one another.
1 Peter 4:10

BREAKING IT DOWN:

\ 'joi-fəl \ 'gi-vər :
exuberantly sharing your joy and gifts with one another are admired or appreciated.

I want to share a friend's story. Whataburger is Wade's favorite restaurant. If you have no idea what I am talking about, Whataburger is a fast food chain restaurant that specializes in (you guessed it) burgers. One day, around Christmas time, Wade was sitting eating his meal when he overheard a couple arguing.

Giving help can spread the love of God.

The girl, who had a Whataburger uniform on, was visibly upset at the guy across from her with his hand on a bag on the table. The guy was so excited because he purchased a pair of maybe $20 skull candy headphones from the gas station that he wanted to give to their son for Christmas. He would get to open a gift this year. The girl was distraught telling the guy he needed to return them because they couldn't afford the headphones and rent, and tried to explain that Christmas isn't about gifts. The couple finished eating and the guy said he would return the headphones, then the girl went back to work.

Wade finished his meal in silence. After throwing his trash away he went out to his car, put $2,000 in an envelope and walked back inside. He walked over to the girl who was standing behind the counter and handed the girl the envelope and said, "Give your son the headphones." Then Wade walked out. As he was getting into his car the girl came running out saying she can't accept the gift. Wade simply said, "Merry Christmas." and kept getting in his car.

The girl started crying and saying thank you over and over again. She told Wade how her 5-year-old boy would have the best Christmas morning getting his head phones, a warm meal, and getting to stay in their apartment for another month. Wade smiled knowing she didn't have to worry for another month and again said, "Merry Christmas, maybe one day you will be able to pay it forward too." This story touched my heart and made me realize I can give gifts, big or small because each one will be used for God's glory.

EXPERIENCE YOUR BEAUTY

Oh, and you don't have to be rich to give to others. Gifts can be your time, talents, or treasures. Spending quality time with someone who is lonely is a gift. Ever helped someone fix something, run an errand for them, or build something? You're using your talents to give to others. Treasure can be things like money, clothes, toys, or anything. Gift giving can make the receiver happy but it also makes the giver happy too.

Did you know that generosity is contagious? Researchers have proven that those who receive gifts are three times more likely to give to others than those who don't receive. God blessed you with many things, so bless others and spread His love. Put love out and it will come back.

TODAY'S PRAYER

Dear Father in heaven, you are Abba, Creator of Heaven and Earth; you created me in your image. Wow. It's incredible. Pour into me today that I may shower those I meet with love. Use me to encourage someone I meet with a smile, a hello, and a kind word. Help me today to shower others with your love. In Jesus' name, amen.

TAKE ACTION

1. What are some specific ways God has blessed you?

2. Why is how we give important?

3. Why does giving with a joyful heart make a difference?

_____

_____

_____

_____

_____

_____

_____

_____

What does the mirror of your heart reflect when you give
joyfully as unto the Lord?

chapter 16

TRUE BEAUTY IS SERVING OTHERS

WHAT GOD IS SAYING ABOUT YOU:

Use whatever gift you have received to serve others.
1 Peter 4:10

BREAKING IT DOWN:

\ 'trü \ 'byü-tē \ 'sər-viŋ \ 'ə-t'hərs :
being in line with the actual state of attributes in a person or item that exalts the mind or spirit or brings delight to the senses, giving two or more people what they need or want.

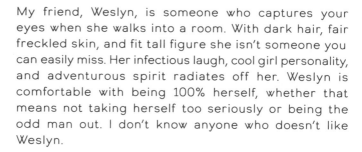

My friend, Weslyn, is someone who captures your eyes when she walks into a room. With dark hair, fair freckled skin, and fit tall figure she isn't someone you can easily miss. Her infectious laugh, cool girl personality, and adventurous spirit radiates off her. Weslyn is comfortable with being 100% herself, whether that means not taking herself too seriously or being the odd man out. I don't know anyone who doesn't like Weslyn.

Whenever I think of Weslyn, her beauty isn't the first thing that comes to mind. I think of her servant heart, for example the way she creates kindness and warmth with true genuineness. I think of how she is everyone's biggest cheerleader, and how she isn't wishing your good fortune was secretly hers. I think of laughing so hard your stomach hurts and how she gives you her direct attention when she's with you. She listens to you and creates memories that last a lifetime. I think of her heart and her service for the Lord.

Weslyn is one of those friends who make life better by simply being in it. She pushes you when you need to be pushed and she is a constant reminder of unconditional love. While Weslyn struggles, makes mistakes, and deals with life issues too, she continues to do her best to help and serve others. She radiates a unique quality that captivates people: living for Jesus.

Helping others shows your true beauty.

Being genuinely happy, supportive, and physically there for others can be hard. But when we live like this Jesus' light shines off of us and to others. It spreads.

Weslyn does her best to serve others with a joyful heart not expecting anything in return. To God and me, this is true beauty.

EXPERIENCE YOUR BEAUTY

Let me, Dr. Lynnette, explain what a servant heart is. Well, someone who has a servant heart puts other people before themselves, they treat others like they want to be treated, and they serve and love without expectation. In Matthew 22:39 Jesus says, 'love your neighbor as you love yourself.' Jesus wants us to care and serve others, not because we have to, but because we want to. Philemon 1:14. 'So that any favor you do would not seem forced but would be voluntary.' This is serving without someone telling you what to do, without a reward, or an expectation of something in return.

Who can have a servant's heart? You can! You can show your love for God by taking care and serving others. It is as easy as smiling at a stranger, checking in on a friend, helping someone with a task, or a compliment. Things like writing an encouraging text, cooking dinner for someone, or visiting someone who is sick all serve the Lord by serving others. You are a woman of true beauty who can radiate Jesus by loving on others with your whole heart.

✝ **TODAY'S PRAYER**

Jesus, sit with me now. Let me feel your embrace as you comfort me with your loving hug. Kindly whisper in my ear who I can help today. When I do, fill me with joy, so your love shines through me. Give me the bold confidence to do this. Let my joy radiate and help me remember this joy of serving others is what truly makes me beautiful and glow. In your name, Amen.

REPEAT IN YOUR MIND & SHINE!

Say over yourself 30x today:

"TRUE BEAUTY is serving others."

TAKE ACTION

1. How can you reflect the beauty of Jesus? Why do others notice that?

2. What is a servant's heart, and how does that affect you and others?

3. What happens when you put Jesus first? How can that change your life?

_____

_____

_____

_____

_____

_____

What does the mirror of your heart reflect about
you serving others?

chapter 17
GIFTS

WHAT GOD IS SAYING ABOUT YOU:

Thanks be to God for his
indescribable gift!
2 Corinthians 9:15

BREAKING IT DOWN:

\ 'gifts :
A noteworthy ability, aptitude, or
endowment; giving; something
voluntarily given by one person to
another without payment.

Since middle school, I have wanted to work in fashion. I wanted to help others experience how clothes could change their mood and/or express their personality. I went to Savannah College of Art and Design and The Fashion Institute of Technology to pursue this dream.

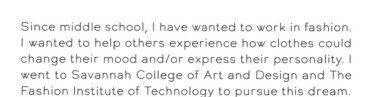

God gives you gifts to serve others.

During one class, I learned how to use programs such as Photoshop, InDesign, Dreamweaver, Illustrator, and more, I had to keep a "blog." It was during this blogging assignment that I discovered my talent for writing. Throughout school, my professors and peers complimented me and encouraged me to write.

One day, I got a call from someone my dad knew: Jenn Gotzon-Chandler. I thought Jenn was going to ask me to lunch or some activity in the city. Instead, she asked me to write for her movie! She explained that God had chosen me. I was filled with excitement to work on a project that highlighted God. I was beginning to love writing.

Months later, I had an opportunity to speak at a charity event. The speech seemed to write itself. After speaking, several people came over to compliment me. I had to tell them God gave me the words. Then I wrote an article about social media and comparison. Again, I was using my writing talent to spread the word of God.

At this very moment, as I sit here sharing all about God's love for you, I am astounded by the gift of writing that He gave me. Instead of fashion, I help write for the healthcare industry. God created my gift of writing to help others in one of the most complicated and critical fields. I, also, get to write for you all. And I know my co-writer, Dr. Lynnette, has a similar story.

I do, Morgan. Let me share how God has given me the gift of writing, even though I am dyslexic. It was difficult for me to read, so I had never read an entire book until I was twenty. In community college, I was diagnosed with dyslexia. I wasn't dumb, I was gifted with a dyslexia brain. Little did I know that there are many amazing people who are dyslexic. After a lot of hard work, I am now a Doctor of Education, a mentor, and an author too. You see, God can use every one of us, in ways we never thought possible, for His kingdom and glory.

EXPERIENCE YOUR BEAUTY

If you begin your journey down one road, don't be discouraged if you take an unexpected turn. God will make sure you get to where you need to be. Hidden talents are not hidden from the Lord. He will bring out the best in you and in surprising ways. Keep your mind and heart open to Him. He has a spectacular life for you, with twists and turns you don't want to miss.

TODAY'S PRAYER

Father in heaven, I praise you because you made me in your image, fearfully and wonderfully made. Thank you. Please show me right now what are the unique gifts you created me with. Kindly show me three of them, realizing kindness is easy to give those around me with a smile. Walk with me hand in hand today as I serve others with those gifts. Thank you, Jesus. Amen.

TAKE ACTION

1. What are the talents you could use for God?

2. What individuals or ministries might need those talents?

3. How can using your talents bring glory to God?

_____

_____

_____

_____

_____

_____

_____

_____

What does the mirror of your heart reflect when you use your gifts and talents for the Lord?

chapter 18
MAKE YOURSELF ATTRACTIVE BY DOING ACTS OF LOVE

WHAT GOD IS SAYING ABOUT YOU:

Your beauty should not come from outward adornment... Rather, it should be that of your inner self, the unfading beauty of a gentle and quiet spirit.
1 Peter 3:3-4

BREAKING IT DOWN:

\ 'māk \ yər-'self \ ə-'trak-tiv \ 'bī \ 'dü-iŋ \ 'akts \ əv \ 'ləv :
to influence, perform an act out of intense love for someone coming from bonds of kinship or personal ties.

Let's face it, girls can be mean. I have been on the receiving end of what people call "girls being girls." I was left out of my friend group because I am a year younger than everyone. When my friends drove around and hung out, I was left sitting at home. Some of these so-called "friends" used me by telling their parents they were hanging me or staying at my home, and found myself writing in my journal talking to God.

I wrote down my prayers, thoughts, feelings, and fears. I leaned on Him to help me during this lonely and confusing time. My relationship with the Lord became deeper and deeper as we spent time together. God was preparing me. Then just like that, I was added to the friend group text! But God was not preparing me to be in the "popular group," He was preparing me to love another who had just been ousted.

A friend had made a mistake by gossiping and was quickly abandoned by these "friends." Within 24 hours she went from being one of the "it" girls to having no friends. I knew what it was like to be on the outside and lonely. God put on my heart to reach out to her. We talked, and I remained her friend. I made sure not to hide my friendship with her, either. We all make mistakes, but God commands us to forgive, show grace, and love one another.

God does things for a reason.

I gave her a journal to write down all of her thoughts and feelings just like I had. I knew I was no better than her, as "he who is without sin, may he cast the first stone." God prepared me in my loneliness, so I could

86

use Him to help another. I got to point my friend to Jesus, just like I did. I got to grow my relationship with Him and with my friend.

EXPERIENCE YOUR BEAUTY

Romans 12:10 says, "Be devoted to one another in love." Friendships are vital in our lives. Healthy relationships help us to feel happy, joy, and acceptance. They can increase your sense of worth, belonging, and feel less lonely. The key word is healthy. Here are some key elements to a healthy relationship: communication, trust, respect, honesty, kindness, forgiveness, empathy, and love. When Jesus commands us to love one another, He wants us to engage in healthy relationships.

But if you're engaged in an unhealthy relationship, then it is time to talk. It is important to remember that hurting people tend to hurt others. So, try to be that girl who talks things out with her friends. Give grace. Be someone who asks if you can help them or are they hurting. When we approach a person with love, they are more likely to share. Maybe you can help them, like Morgan did with her friend. With Love.

TODAY'S PRAYER

Our Lord in heaven, we realize you do things for a reason. I don't understand why my heart hurts at school or when I browse because of the negative things I experience. Calm my anxious mind to know you are in charge of everything. Help me see from your eyes. Comfort me now. Let me feel your peace today. Overflow me with your love. Heal my aching heart. In the name of Jesus.

TAKE ACTION

1. How can you pay attention when God nudges you to show love to someone?

2. Why are acts of love attractive?

3. Why is it important to serve others with joy?

_____

_____

_____

_____

_____

_____

_____

What does the mirror of your heart reflect you doing acts of love toward others?

I AM A
OBEDIENT TO
MY CALLING

"Plans to prosper you and not to harm you."
Jeremiah 29:11

I am COURAGEOUS.
I am OBEDIENT TO MY CALLING.

God gives me talents for his glory.
With God all things are possible.
God has plans to prosper me.
God has plans not to harm me.

OBEDIENT TO MY CALLING

chapter 19

COURAGEOUS

WHAT GOD IS SAYING ABOUT YOU:

Be strong and courageous. Do not be afraid or terrified because of them, for the Lord your God goes with you; he will never leave you nor forsake you.
Deuteronomy 31:6

BREAKING IT DOWN:

\ kə-'rā-jəs : possessing or being marked by mental or moral bravery to risk, persist, and overcome danger, fear, or challenge.

I have never liked the spotlight. I don't like people's attention on me because I have a fear that I will mess up; say the wrong thing, act the wrong way, or not be who they want me to be. For years, I have always put on a "show" to be who someone else wants me to be... and never really been completely myself. I let myself be put in a box of parameters of what others wanted. I thought this would be best, that I would be the girl who everyone else wanted me to be.

They wanted me to listen to their problems while they dumped their heaviness onto my shoulders, but they didn't see that I couldn't lift anymore. They wanted me to not stand up for myself or challenge opinions, but they didn't know it chipped away at my soul. They wanted me to look a certain way so that I fit in with their looks, but they didn't realize I was uncomfortable. They wanted me to partake in activities I had no joy in so they didn't feel uncomfortable in their decisions, but they didn't care about the anxiety it caused.

One day I looked in the mirror and completely broke down. I didn't recognize the girl staring back at me. How could I have? The reflection in the mirror was made up of a little bit of everyone else. I didn't like the clothes I wore in order to fit in, I didn't recognize the lack of passion for what I did every day, and I didn't agree with the person I had become. But this is what everyone else wanted me to right? If I did what they wanted me to then how could they not like me?

You get strength from God.

God didn't put me or you on this Earth to be a replica of someone else. He put you here to be you, and he put me here to be me. Even though I didn't feel like myself because I wasn't being authentically me, God never abandoned me on my journey to finding myself. He gave me the strength to pull myself out of the darkness and the courage to be myself. I was so focused on wanting to be liked by others that I didn't realize I didn't like myself.

EXPERIENCE YOUR BEAUTY

The funny thing is, my relationships are stronger than ever when I am myself. The feeling of always questioning who you are can only go on for so long. I set boundaries with people and worked on finding who I am. This didn't happen overnight. It took a lot of trial and error. It took long conversations and prayers with the Lord to get to where I am today. I asked Him for help. Isaiah 40:29-31 states that God will carry you when you have no strength left. He did exactly that and gave me the courage to be authentically me

TODAY'S PRAYER

Hi Jesus! How are you? Thank you for listening to me pray today. I love you. Fill me with your strength as if I am a container of water overflowing. Let me go into all I do feeling strong and courageous. Holding tightly onto you as you lead me fearlessly through the mess. Turn my mess into a message for your glory. I love you, Jesus. Amen.

REPEAT IN YOUR MIND & SHINE!

Say over yourself 30x today:

"I AM courageous."

TAKE ACTION

1. How has fear kept you from stepping out in faith?

2. Why is prayer so important as you step out in faith to chase your dreams for God?

3. How can faith in God and courage equip you to become the beautiful woman of faith God desires you to be?

What does the mirror of your heart reflect about
you becoming courageous?

chapter 20

OBEDIENT TO MY CALLING

WHAT GOD IS SAYING ABOUT YOU:

I have raised you up for this very purpose, that I might show you my power and that my name might be proclaimed.
Exodus 9:16

BREAKING IT DOWN:

| \ ō-'bē-dē-ənt | tú | \ 'mī | \ 'ko-liŋ: conforming to God's orders to signify that I am moving toward a strong inner urge to choose a specific course of action, accompanied by a belief in divine intervention.

Have you ever told God no? I have.

In 2018, I was invited to speak at a charity event for type one diabetes. Immediately, I said, no. The event was expecting about 1000 people. Being vulnerable is not my strong suit, and taking the stage to talk about my health struggles was not for me. But God had other plans.

For 5 days straight, He spoke to me in a dream. I was standing on stage with a spotlight on me, and I kept hearing, "You're speaking at this year's event." I'd wake up and say no, again and again. God was insistent. He started speaking to me, through the Holy Spirit, when I was awake too. "You're speaking at this year's event." Finally, against my desire and my fears, I called and told them, "I'm in."

Follow God's calling for you.

Once I accepted, God began downloading the speech to me. Sounds weird, right? He gave me every word for my speech, through more dreams, while showering, and even at the grocery store. Every word kept flowing, until I wrote down exactly what I was going to say. I practiced my speech about five times. While I did prepare, it was clear that God was doing the work, I was simply His vessel.

I don't remember much of the event. I was scared and nervous. When I was called up, I walked on stage, a bright spotlight was on me - it was exactly my dream! I took a deep breath...that's all I remember. In the audience, my mom told me, "It looked like something came over you." The room was silent, through the entire speech, as people listened. I snapped back, after my speech, to the realization that the Holy Spirit had just taken over me. The audience was in tears.

After my speech, I had the opportunity to share more about diabetes AND about Jesus. People asked me how I wrote such a beautiful speech and all I could reply was, "God gave it to me." We raised $1.8 million, that night.

EXPERIENCE YOUR BEAUTY

Walking with Jesus means you have the Holy Spirit in you. Talking to you. Some people call this intuition, but we know it's God. Obeying our intuition, the Holy Spirit, can save us from many hardships, hurt relationships, struggles, and bring us joy, peace, and closer to Him.

Obeying doesn't have to be something big, like a speaking engagement; we can obey Him throughout our daily lives. Like when He asks us to help and care for one another. Take the time to listen, before you make decisions because sometimes it's a yes from God, even when you think it's a no. Step out in faith and confidence, and God will provide the rest.

TODAY'S PRAYER

Lord, you have plans to prosper me and not to harm me. Help me nestle this truth deep, deep inside my heart. Show me the mountain ahead you want me to conquer. When you walk with me, You are the light upon my path on every step I take. I thank you. For this step makes me beautiful. Glorious because I am walking into the calling you created me for. Amen Jesus.

REPEAT IN YOUR MIND & SHINE!
Say over yourself 30x today:

"I AM obedient to my calling."

TAKE ACTION

1. Has God ever called you to do something you didn't want to do? Did you obey him?

2. How does being obedient to your calling affect you and others?

_____

_____

_____

_____

_____

_____

_____

_____

What does the mirror of your heart reflect when you are obedient to your calling?

chapter 21

GOD GIVES TALENTS
FOR HIS GLORY

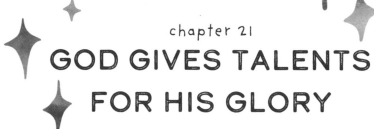

WHAT GOD IS SAYING ABOUT YOU:

His master replied, 'Well done, good
and faithful servant! You have been
faithful with a few things; I will put
you in charge of many things.
Matthew 25:21

BREAKING IT DOWN:

| \ 'päd | \ 'givs | \ 'ta-lənts | \ fər |
\ (h)iz,| \ 'glor-ē : Athletic, artistic,
or creative talent are gifts from our
Lord that have a purpose and are intended
for worshipful adoration and praise.

The words "I'm not...enough" enter my mind more often than I'd like to admit. I'm not fit enough to do that workout class. I'm not pretty enough for him to want me. I'm not smart enough to talk about politics. I'm not witty enough for this game. I'm not wise enough to share my knowledge. I'm not capable enough to express God's love. I'm not trained enough to write to the masses. I am not enough.

You are enough with God, He gives you talents.

Sometimes I focus too much on what others think of me. I don't want to be a burden so I don't share my thoughts, feelings, or problems. As a people pleaser, I tend to hold myself back and try to just conform to those around me. All of this is exhausting because I'm not being me. No one tells you that finding who you are takes a while, and that's okay.

Each and every one of us are constantly changing and evolving and that usually happens when we feel uncomfortable. That's why I am sitting here writing a book sharing about the love of Jesus and that you don't have to earn HIS love. It scares me to write my thoughts, feelings, stories, and put myself out there because this isn't natural for me.

I finally learned that when I hear, "I'm not enough" it comes from this world we live in and NOT from God. When those negative messages are repeating and crushing my soul, I know I haven't been spending time with God. I am slowly understanding that He didn't call me to be perfect or liked by everyone, He called me to be near Him and to listen to His words.

EXPERIENCE YOUR BEAUTY

Romans 12:2 tells us to not conform to the patterns of this world but be transformed by the renewing of your mind and then you will be able to test and approve what God's will is. The second part is fully contingent on the first part. You have to keep renewing yourself - reading His word, worshiping Him, surrounding yourself with the right people. Then you will know when to say yes, when to walk away, when to make that big move, or any other life decision. Keep growing with God, and listen to what He is telling you.

Renewing your mind and finding your talents will transform your life. A positive attitude practicing your talents, and focusing on His promises to you WILL transform your life. How do you get started? Open the Bible. Read for yourself. Join a Bible study at a local church. Not for you, too scary? YouTube it! Yes, technology can be used for good. Look up the Bible Project to give you a better understanding of the Bible. Find your local church online and watch service from your own home. Take a step towards Love. You are worthy of reaching out and asking God for understanding, wisdom, and love.

TODAY'S PRAYER

Dear Jesus, today my heart is hurting, and I need you to lift me up. Whisper in my soul the talents you have made me with. Remind me that my smile is enough. Help me see myself as you created me. Give me the strength today to use my gifts to love others as you love me. In your precious name, Amen.

REPEAT IN YOUR MIND & SHINE!

Say over yourself 30x today:

"GOD GIVES talents for His glory."

TAKE ACTION

1. Why is it so scary to step out in faith?

2. How are you renewing your mind?

3. What talents has God given to you? How can you use those talents for him?

_____

_____

_____

_____

_____

_____

_____

_____

What does the mirror of your heart reflect about using your talents for God?

chapter 22
WITH GOD ALL THINGS ARE POSSIBLE

WHAT GOD IS SAYING ABOUT YOU:

Humanly speaking, it is impossible.
But with God everything is possible.
Matthew 19:26

BREAKING IT DOWN:

\ 'with | \ 'gäd | \ 'ol | \ 'thiŋs | \ 'er
| \ 'pä-sə-bəl : Every concrete entity
can be thought of, done, or occur in
response to nature, tradition, or
manners in an action from our Abba
Father, Creator of Heaven and Earth.

Impossible is usually some big obstacle in life that seems too difficult, challenging, or insurmountable... but not for my friend Jacquelyn. She is one of my best friends, and has type one diabetes, just like me. She was told that having an autoimmune illness would limit her activities and her life. Simple things like running a mile, eating carbs or sweets, or even exercising.

Before she got diagnosed, she played sports and was into fitness. Once she got sick, she used it as an excuse not to strive for the things she really wanted. She was angry, confused, and scared. She thought the life she envisioned was being taken away. For years Jacquelyn believed her illness stood in the way of things she wanted to do and the dreams she had. Then Jacquelyn discovered cycling!

Class after class, she began to wonder if she could teach the class. "Why not me? Why couldn't I do that?" Jacquelyn asked herself. Little by little she gained the confidence, motivation, and training to teach her first cycling class. Now with over 500 fitness classes under her belt, Jacquelyn realized she had done the impossible. She had proved others wrong!

With God all things are possible.

When Jacquelyn first got sick she thought her life had been taken from her, but slowly she realized that the truth in Philippians 4:13. "I can do all things through him who gives me strength." She did wonder why God gave her such an "impossible" thing to live with, and the answer is, so we give Him the glory and lean on Him. Jacquelyn learned to trust in Him, and the more she did the more she realized it was never an impossible dream for God.

EXPERIENCE YOUR BEAUTY

Little by little you too can achieve your goals. According to researchers, goal setting helps you focus on what is important. It can help you stay motivated. Goals help you guide your life towards the activities, classes, universities, and careers you may have. Setting goals can help make you decisions, discover obstacles, visualize your future, and even help you create a more positive environment for yourself. Your dreams are within your reach for nothing is impossible WITH God.

Remember to tell God what you want and ask Him to guide you towards His plans for you.

Lean in to Him and use these tips to help you reach your dreams. Write your dreams down; you can use a journal, dream board, or just a post-it note list. Take each item and break it down to doable tasks. Take-action, be consistent, and track your progress. Finally, celebrate the small successes along the way. God's plans for you are never impossible.

TODAY'S PRAYER

Wow Lord. What a concept. Help me truly believe that with you, all things are possible. Reconstruct my mind to see opportunities around me as a way you can move mountains. Open my eyes throughout today to grasp this truth. With You, all things are possible. Show me something that I can believe you for. In your name Jesus, Amen.

REPEAT IN YOUR MIND & SHINE!

Say over yourself 30x today:

"WITH GOD all things are possible."

TAKE ACTION

1. What are some seemingly impossible situations in your life?

2. Why do you focus on your limited abilities instead of God's limitless ones?

3. How can your faith exceed your fears?

_____

_____

_____

_____

_____

_____

_____

What does the mirror of your heart reflect when you truly
realize that nothing is impossible for God?

chapter 23

GOD HAS PLANS TO PROSPER ME

WHAT GOD IS SAYING ABOUT YOU:

For I know the plans I have for you, declares the Lord, plans to prosper you and not to harm you, plans to give you hope and a future.
Jeremiah 29:11

BREAKING IT DOWN:

\ 'gäd | \ 'haz | \ 'plans | \ tə | \ 'prä-spər | \ 'mē : Abba Father holds and maintains your privileges and entitlements, a carefully thought-out plan of action or goal signaling direction to succeed in an endeavor.

In today's world, we see success as money and lavish lifestyles. This viewpoint causes us to lose track of God's blessings. Blessings can be your talents, surroundings, location, peers, family, and yes, even money. But sometimes we miss our blessings when we compare ourselves. Sometimes, I find myself comparing my life to others. This person is younger or makes more money than me. Their life is all together, happy, and in a relationship. I think I know them, but I really have no idea. I assume their life is perfect from their posts.

Constantly comparing shifts your focus and you forget what you do have. Personally, God has blessed me with a strong support system, personal strength, a roof over my head, and so much more. I have to remember that God may have a different plan for me versus others, and I am exactly where I am supposed to be.

Scroll, double tap, repeat. Social media is a blessing and a curse. We are constantly exposed to edited and curated lifestyles that seem both attainable and not. You might get motivated, but then beat yourself up because you begin negative self-talk. I'm not doing enough, pretty or talented enough. Especially in social media, we tend to see the end result, not the process or hard work it took to get there. Everyone has something they are struggling with, just like I do.

> Instead of seeing what you don't have, count your blessings.

I would like to challenge you. Next time you are comparing yourself...take a step back. Write down your blessings, what do you have? This will shift the narrative from negative to positive. Then thank the Lord for all He has given you. Use your blessings to spread His love. I have learned that it is more important for me to follow the Lord than follow people I don't know and who don't know me on social media.

EXPERIENCE YOUR BEAUTY

To succeed, prosper, or thrive can mean many different things for each of us. Here are some truths about success...always do YOUR best, try to understand the difference between need and want. Believe in the Lord and yourself. Life comes in seasons, each one with its own rewards. Love what you do. Take care of yourself, and sometimes that means saying no. Gratitude needs to be practiced, daily. Each struggle is a badge of honor and healing from it is thriving. Don't give up, small wins are still wins...enjoy each one. The most prosperous lives are filled with love, love yourself and loving others.

God wants to give you the best, always. He says so! Proverbs 11:25 says, "the generous man will be prosperous." 2 Kings 18:7, also says that when the Lord is with her, wherever she goes she will prosper. Immediately, slowly, or tentatively, it will happen, He promises.

TODAY'S PRAYER

Dear Lord, remind me today of five things I should be grateful for. Show them right now to me. Please help me think about these beautiful blessings all day today, especially when I am feeling down and insecure. Remind me that when I think on things good, pure, and lovely, you uplift my soul. Thank you, Jesus, for being my Savior and rooting for me. Amen.

REPEAT IN YOUR MIND & SHINE!

Say over yourself 30x today:

"GOD HAS PLANS to prosper me."

TAKE ACTION

1. Why do you sometimes fail to see the blessings God has given you?

2. What are some of the ways God has made you wealthy?

3. How can prosperity be used for God?

_____

_____

_____

_____

_____

_____

_____

What does the mirror of your heart reflect when you realize God wants you to prosper?

chapter 24

GOD HAS PLANS NOT TO HARM ME

WHAT GOD IS SAYING ABOUT YOU:

I can do all things through Christ
which strengtheneth me.
Philippians 4:13

BREAKING IT DOWN:

\ 'gäd \ 'haz \ 'plans \ 'nät \ tə \
'härm \ 'mē : God offers a strategy
for reaching a purpose, suggesting
direction that won't harm the person
or people being addressed physically
or psychologically.

The high school I went to was competitive, academically and with extra-curricular activities. School wasn't easy for me. While I loved having a piece of paper that told me exactly how to get an A, I had to study and work hard. I was the captain of the cheer squad, a PAL (a mentoring program for young kids), in the National Honor Society, involved in Student Council, a member of YoungLife, and much more. With all of this, I never felt like I was good or capable enough. I felt that if I didn't go to certain colleges, then I would be a failure. If I didn't measure up to my brother by getting into the University of Texas or going to an equal school, I was somehow lesser in value.

> Things won't always go the way you want them to, but God knows what's best.

God had other plans for me. Instead of going to a major university, I went to art school. The Lord called me to Savannah College of Art and Design; and then, He called me to The Fashion Institute of Technology. I knew I wasn't supposed to go to a traditional college. Telling my family that I didn't want to do something "traditional" was hard. Going against the "norm" is hard. I feared letting my parent's down and not living up to other people's expectations of me. The amazing thing I learned was - I don't have to live up to others' expectations of me, I just need to live for God. Knowing God was beside me every step of the way made the journey easier.

EXPERIENCE YOUR BEAUTY

God truly has a path for you. Even if it doesn't make sense right now, you'll be able to look back on your story and see where He has guided you to your future and unique calling. Life isn't a straight path, it has curves, mountains, deep valleys, deserts, and forests that you might not be able to appreciate until you have gone through them. Once I handed over my fear of the future I was able to see the future He wants for me, and it's amazing and one I could have never dreamed of. Trust Him.

High school is just one of many challenging times you will face. The Lord does not promise to remove you from all trials and tribulations, quite the opposite. He will walk with you through each and every one of them. One thing you must ALWAYS remember, life is constantly changing. As you grow, new experiences will strengthen you, even though they may feel like they are crushing you.

Tell yourself that YOU WILL BE OK. Things WILL change. You WILL prosper from this experience. Allow each experience to shape you, prosper you, and grow you into a woman filled with His love, grace, and wisdom. Jeremiah 19:12-13 says that all we need to do is to call on Him, seek Him in prayer, and He will listen to you.

TODAY'S PRAYER

Father in Heaven, Abba Father, draw my heart closest to your love right now. Lemme feel your presence surround me. Allow all distractions to vanish, and let me focus on you. Comfort my aching heart, and let me desire your will for my every move. Lord, carry me today. In your name, Jesus. Amen.

TAKE ACTION

1. Why does God want you to be successful?

2. Why do you never have to worry about God harming you?

3. Are there any points in your life that you can see looking back that God has guided you down your path?

_____

_____

_____

_____

_____

_____

_____

_____

What does the mirror of your heart reflect when you realize God's plans are not meant to harm you?

OPEN MY HEART

" Dear Jesus, Help me grasp how wide,
long, high & deep is your love for me."
Ephesians 3:18

Open MY HEART.
Jesus, MY FRIEND.
Jesus, MY SAVIOR.

Help me comprehend
your love for me.
Help me grasp how wide, long,
high, and deep your love is for me.
I am beautiful for your purpose.

OPEN
MY HEART

chapter 25

OPEN MY HEART

WHAT GOD IS SAYING ABOUT YOU:

Create in me a clean heart, O God,
and renew a right spirit within me.
Psalm 51:10

BREAKING IT DOWN:

\ 'ō-pən \ 'mī \ 'härt : not being
enclosed or constrained by any barrier:
able to be accessed from all or virtually
all sides, not sealed or locked referring
to me or myself with courage or vigor, one's
innermost feelings or impulses.

Taking pictures is an entire activity for my friends and me. Our "session" goes like this–take a couple pictures, look for flaws, take more, adjust angles, take more, we don't like our hair, take more, the background is wrong, take more. There is a lot of fine tuning and adjustments to get the picture we like. We do these fixes and evaluations all the time with our outer appearances. But why do we often neglect checking in with ourselves and adjusting our inner beauty?

Open your heart to God.

In those quiet moments with God, I know my weaknesses and things I need to work on to fix. But because they aren't visible, I sometimes overlook and forget about them. The Lord will keep reminding me that I need to work on them. For me, my inner beauty is the way I show up for my friends, but for a long time I overbooked myself so much that I wasn't giving anyone my best, not even myself. My time was so overbooked, that I had no spontaneous time or time for my own self-care.

The word "no" has slowly entered my vocabulary. Knowing I wasn't showing up at my best helped me to change. Unlike visual appearance, inner beauty doesn't normally have a quick fix solution. It takes time, but my friend, you are not alone.

As one of our teen editors said, "I feel like we often overlook our inner issues. We tend to sort of block them out, and if someone does call us out - we ignore it. But when we do accept our internal issues, it may be hard to change them, especially if they have become habits. Sometimes, instead of being open, we try to hide. But when it comes to God, He already knows the issues we face and wants to help us overcome them with no judgment. I just think that's amazing."

EXPERIENCE YOUR BEAUTY

Being open is being vulnerable, which can bring some uncertainty. A person's willingness to accept the emotional risk comes with the great possibility of love and being loved. Past hurt, current pain, and fear can stop us from becoming vulnerable. But when we move past the hurt, pain, and/or fear, we build trust. Opening our hearts allows us to build intimate relationships and increase our self-worth. It's a complete circle. Opening our heart to the Lord will allow Him to help us break free from whatever negative issues we have, so we can see what He sees in us.

To open your heart to the Lord, let Him into your every day. Let Him have time to talk to you through scripture, praise music, or through the wisdom of others. Open your heart to the possibility that you are more than your outer looks. He knows you intimately and loves you deeply. When you give Him your heart, He will show you what HE sees. Your true beauty.

TODAY'S PRAYER

Wow, Jesus, I never realized I block my heart from feeling. It is a protection for me. Let me nestle into your loving hands for my protection. Open my heart in your name Jesus. Fill my heart with forgiveness. Fill my heart with trust in you. Fill my heart with your peace. Fill my heart with strength. Let me hold onto your hand with an open heart. Amen.

TAKE ACTION

1. Do you know of anything God is trying to help you fix?

2. Why does he want you to open your heart to him?

3. How does it make you feel when you close your heart to God? How do you feel when you open it to him?

_____

_____

_____

_____

_____

_____

_____

_____

What does the mirror of your heart reflect when you ask God to open your heart?

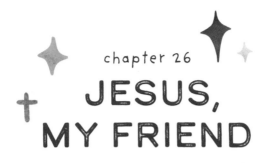

chapter 26
JESUS, MY FRIEND

WHAT GOD IS SAYING ABOUT YOU:

I have called you friends, for everything that I learned from my Father I have made known to you.
John 15:15

BREAKING IT DOWN:

\ 'jē-zəs \ 'mī \ 'frend :
Relationship between me and the Son of God who gave his life in sacrifice for me.

Have you ever met someone and instantly felt like you have known each other your entire lives? You can just look at each other and start laughing because you know exactly what they are thinking. This connection goes beyond just having the same interest or being in the same grade. This is a soul connection. It's what I call a soul sister.

My friend Jacquelyn is one of my soul sisters. We immediately hit it off because we are both type one diabetics, with similar personalities, and many of the same interests. However, our friendship goes beyond surface-level. Jacquelyn and I have gone through highs and lows together. Even living in different states, she has always been there for me. She will drop everything if I need a shoulder to cry on, scream into the abyss with me, and eat cake with me to celebrate. She inspires me to be my authentic-self and she has saved me from myself more times than I can count. She encourages me, pushes me, and makes me a better person. But I have one friend who is even better than her... Jesus.

Your best friend is Jesus.

Jesus brings me peace. He settles my soul with faint whispers of reassurance and everlasting love. When I feel anxious, He is there telling me we've got you-don't worry. When I feel not good enough, He reminds me that I am enough for Him. When I think about the future, He speaks that He has plans for me. But just like with Jacquelyn, the friendship is a two-way relationship. I have to put effort into both relationships by spending time, listening, communicating, and loving both of them.

EXPERIENCE YOUR BEAUTY

I, Dr. Lynnette, have soul sisters too. I love what a teen editors said about a friend who is closer than a soul sister/brother. "We have to grow that relationship with God by praying, worshiping, and reading the Bible. Like any friendship, we have to get to know Him better. I feel like everyone, nowadays, is trying to find that perfect best friend that they have seen in the movies or that friend you can tell everything to and not everyone finds that friend. But what they don't realize is God is right there ready to be your friend, your best friend, and I think that's so great and is what has helped me with the loneliness that I have felt."

Friends will come into our lives for a 'reason,' a 'season,' or they may become 'life-long'. A friend for a 'reason' could be someone you're in the same class, while a friend for a 'season' could be a sports teammate, but 'life-long' friends travel with you past the reason or season. They are rare; however, we will always have a LIFE-long friend in Jesus. God yearns for a relationship with us from the moment He created us in our mother's womb and walks with us for our whole life. Even when we neglect our relationship, He is always with us.

TODAY'S PRAYER

Dear Jesus, sometimes I feel lonely and want to get comfort in my heart from you. You are my friend; help me see and believe you to be my best friend. A best friend who plays songs of worship in my heart, a best friend who sings delight over my looks, a best friend who makes me roar with laughter from joy, walk hand-in-hand with me today, Jesus, as my best friend. Amen.

REPEAT IN YOUR MIND & SHINE!

Say over yourself 30x today:

"JESUS, you are my friend."

TAKE ACTION

1. Do you have a soul sister? How does your relationship look and is it similar to your relationship with Jesus?

2. What does it mean to you to have Jesus as your friend?

3. How can you be a good friend to him and how can you allow him to take the lead in your friendship?

_____

_____

_____

_____

_____

_____

_____

_____

What does it mean to the mirror of your heart to have Jesus as your personal friend?

chapter 27

JESUS, MY SAVIOR

WHAT GOD IS SAYING ABOUT YOU:

No one has greater love [nor stronger commitment] than to lay down his own life for his friends.
John 15:13

BREAKING IT DOWN:

\ ˈjē-zəs | \ ˈmī | sav·ior | \ ˈsāv-yər: one who delivers salvation from peril or destruction.

In the year 2020 the entire world shut down. A global pandemic caused chaos among many, stopping all of us from everyday life. We were all told to hang on tight for two weeks. Two weeks turned into two months which turned into six months, until the world stopped spinning for a year.

Everyone in the world had to slow down and take a minute to breathe. Jesus' prayer line was ringing off the hook with the uncertainties caused by COVID and the effects it caused friends, families, and communities. Olivia was one of the many who was confused on why Jesus had turned the world upside down.

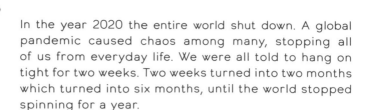

God will never leave your side.

Olivia and her sister are both a part of the arts community: performing is in their souls. Both girls got a front row seat experience of the Broadway shutdown causing the art community to fall apart quickly. Thousands of performers and those who work in the entertainment industry lost their only form of income within the matter of minutes.

One of those people was a dear family friend. She and her husband, who was also involved in Broadway, had to find another way to keep a roof over their heads. At such a devastating time where everything Olivia had known was about to cease to exist, she, admittedly, began to doubt Jesus. How does He simply stand by and watch our family members, friends, and communities suffer?

In the waiting for life to get back to normal, Olivia filled

124

her time with what fueled her soul: performing. She enrolled in dance classes and voice lessons, participated in concerts, and organized fundraisers. She auditioned from her bedroom and participated in several performances organized by her school. Olivia was passing the time but didn't realize that there were millions of other kids and adults doing the same thing - aimlessly doing what they loved strictly because they loved it.

EXPERIENCE YOUR BEAUTY

In the moments of forced rest that Jesus provided us, people found their purpose and passion again. Jesus stopped the world so we could shift and focus on what really matters: HIM. Waiting is an important part of following Christ, because 'in the waiting' is where faith comes in. Even when Jesus shakes the world like a snow globe, He will make sure His light continues to burn for all to see. Many didn't have time to put into Jesus because of their busy schedules. Well, He made time.

Savior, you have given us such a blessing when the world stopped. In that time, many of us were allowed to deepen our passions, focus on our families, discover new things, and rest. Thank you, Lord, for saving us.

TODAY'S PRAYER

Hi Jesus, good morning, goodnight, good day. Be with me. Let me know your deep calls to deep that you will never leave me, that you walk beside me through all waters of hope and turmoil. Hold my hand right now, let me feel your presence. Let me choose to hold your hand throughout today, reminding myself you will never leave my side. I love you, Jesus. Thank you. In your name, I pray, Amen.

REPEAT IN YOUR MIND & SHINE!

Say over yourself 30x today:

"JESUS, my savior."

TAKE ACTION

1. Have you ever doubted Jesus? If so, what helped you through that time of doubt?

2. How has Jesus helped preserve the light in your community?

3. In what ways has He earned the title of your Savior?

_____

_____

_____

_____

_____

_____

_____

_____

What does the mirror of your heart reflect about having Jesus as your Savior?

chapter 28
FORGIVE ME

WHAT GOD IS SAYING ABOUT YOU:

Bear with each other and forgive one another if any of you has a grievance against someone.
Colossians 3:13

BREAKING IT DOWN:

/fərg'iv/ | /mē/ : surrender your pain and anger toward someone through Jesus.

We are no longer limited. Nowadays packages get delivered in one-two days. We can get any type of food delivered in about an hour. We can watch an entire season of our favorite show in one sitting. We have access to the world at our fingertips with our cellphones and the internet. We have libraries filled with books, stores filled with clothes and food, and products from around the world. We can have friends next door or across the ocean. Our lives are limitless and this is both a blessing and a curse.

> No matter how much you've sinned,
> God will forgive you.

Life can be overwhelming. So many decisions and problems, and each one seems life altering. We face problems with family, friends, and our communities. Also, all of these possibilities create temptations which cause us to stumble and sometimes do the wrong things. With each thought of doubt and distance from God, we may feel like we are unworthy of Jesus and His forgiveness, but thankfully we are not.

A teen editor's story: "when my parents got divorced, it was hard. We stopped going to church. My mom was sad, my dad was gone, and I felt so alone. I started questioning why God would allow this to happen. If he loves me so much why did he let this happen. I stopped praying, worshiping and anything related to God.

After a year and a half without God I was lonely. I thought He left me. I was wrong. He never left me. He sent someone to help me go. He sent Pastor Ivan. Ivan is a dear friend to my family. He told us he was starting a new church and invited us. I was weary about going because I felt so much shame and guilt. Fortunately, Ivan reminded me that God sent His one and only son, Jesus, to pay for all our sins. God loves us so much He sent HIS son. He didn't have to, but He did because he loves us."

One of my mentors gave me this analogy about our lives here on Earth and how we see sin, shortcomings, and mistakes. We see each sin head on. Think of a stack of Oreos. Us humans tend to see ourselves and others head on; every fault adding another Oreo to the stack. One on top of another, building higher and higher...10, 20, 100. But God looks at us and our stack of Oreos (sin) from a bird's eye view – He only sees one Oreo no matter how tall the stack.

EXPERIENCE YOUR BEAUTY

He is limitless with His love, grace, mercy, and forgiveness. Limitless with His desire for us to know Him and be with Him forever. Romans 8:38-39 tells us that there is nothing that can separate us from God's love. It is truly unconditional and forever. He sees everything, and loves us. Just as our world may seem like it has no limits, God is the one who is truly limitless.

TODAY'S PRAYER

Wow, Lord, Father in heaven. Sometimes the anguish over my belly where I hold my pain causes me to stir with an ever-going uneasy restlessness. See me here, right now. I know you see me; help me see you. As I take a breath in and let it out, encourage me to give my sin to you and believe you forgive. Help me turn from my wrong-doing and reach for your hand, Amen.

TAKE ACTION

1. Why do you need God's love, mercy, and forgiveness?

2. How does it make you feel that no matter what God loves you?

3. How can you switch the narrative from seeing a stack of oreos to seeing it from bird's eye view?

_____

_____

_____

_____

_____

_____

_____

_____

How does it affect the mirror of your heart to find freedom in forgiving yourself and those who have hurt you?

chapter 29

GRASP YOUR LOVE

WHAT GOD IS SAYING ABOUT YOU:

And may you have the power to understand, as all God's people should, how wide, how long, how high, and how deep his love is.
Ephesians 3:18-19

BREAKING IT DOWN:

/wīd/ /äNG/ /hī/ /dēp/ /yo͝or/ / ləv/ /fər/ /'mē : How far-reaching upward and deeply focused within God's love is for me.

Birthdays are one of my favorite holidays. I'm not the biggest fan of my birthday, but other people's birthdays are something I look forward to. My friends Brittany and Rose do event planning for a living, so we go all out with a theme, decor, cake, props, and gifts. They are really good at making memories for even the smallest moments. I mean even our book clubs have a theme, decor, and little finishes that push it over the top. Events are how they show love, and they were made to do it.

My favorite part about birthday parties isn't the theme, the decor, or the little details. While those do make the experience better, my favorite part is actually when the candles are lit and friends and family are belting out the traditional happy birthday song. The way someone glows in that moment when they look out and see the people who love them have gathered around and are pouring that love into them, is similar to seeing a bride on her wedding day. You just glow when you're surrounded by love.

The way Brittany and Rose can elevate a small occasion into an event because they are masters at their skills, is nothing compared to what God can do. Think of God's love. Try and grasp the depth of His love for us. It's bigger than those glowing moments; it's eternal. God is THE MASTER at His craft and He made you.

God's love is unconditional.

God wants to celebrate the special beauty in each of us. Not the beauty on the outside, but the amazing skills, talents, passions, and characteristics that we have on the inside. God's love in us allows us to glow. His love glows through our loving hearts and helping hands. Our beauty began when He created us and lives eternal.

EXPERIENCE YOUR BEAUTY

Researchers define unconditional love as affection without any conditions or limitations. It is offered without strings attached and given freely. You don't base your love on what another can give you, do for you, or what you might get in return. You simply love, want the best for the other person, and want them happy more than you want it for yourself. This is known as Agape love.

Scripture tells us that agape love comes from God, is God, and is all God wants for us. When we have Jesus in our hearts and we share love, we are sharing agape love. That's the beauty we have inside us that glows when we love one another. 1 John 4:8 says, whoever does not love does not know God, because God is love. It may be cliché, but all we need is love...God's love.

TODAY'S PRAYER

Hi Jesus, sit next to me right now. Open my eyes to see you, truly see you sitting next to me as my best friend. Encourage me to live my dreams, the calling you put inside me. Overwhelm me with your never-ending love. Pouring into every crevice of my body, soaking up my sin with forgiveness. Overflow me with your porridge of unconditional love. Help me to believe and reach for your heart within my hand, Amen.

REPEAT IN YOUR MIND & SHINE!

Say over yourself 30x today:

"HELP ME grasp
how wide, long, high &
deep your love is for me."

TAKE ACTION

1. God says he knit you together in your mother's womb. What does that mean to you?

2. How does the touch of the Master's hand make a difference?

3. What do you think is beautiful about God?

_____

_____

_____

_____

_____

_____

_____

How does it affect the mirror of your heart when you truly get the scope of God's love for you?

chapter 30

MY PURPOSE

WHAT GOD IS SAYING ABOUT YOU:

For we are God's masterpiece. He has
created us anew in Christ
Jesus, so we can do the good things
he planned for us long ago.
Ephesians 2:10

BREAKING IT DOWN:

\ 'mī | pur·pose \ 'pər-pəs : referring
to myself in particular as agent,
objective of a behavior, or close
friend to designate as a goal for oneself.

I love hearing people's stories. It is inspiring to hear how someone's life made a dramatic turn for the better. My mom graduated with a degree in finance; but, what does she do for a living now? She runs and operates nursing homes.

God has a purpose for you.

When I asked my mom why she worked at the nursing home, she told me that she had a calling to help people. These homes are not glamorous, and no one has "being in a nursing home" on their bucket list. She wants to bring light to a dark time in many people's lives -this is what she was called to do, this is her purpose.

I went to fashion school for advertising, marketing, and communications. In high school, I would have told you I would be working in the fashion industry. However, I have a calling to writing and helping people in their time of need. I work in HR in the healthcare industry. God has called me where he needed me and it could change down the road. Right now, though, I use my words to not only help others, but also to share Jesus.

Dr. Lynnette here: Thinking about your life calling may seem overwhelming, but you don't have to worry about it. As one editor shared, "dramatic changes in one's life are completely normal, and should not be feared," because God has a plan for you. Plans to prosper you, to bring you hope, and a future, so you cannot mess it up.

This is a time of exploration, a time to learn, be open, make discoveries, and nothing will be wasted. So, follow your dreams, start with that major, take that class, and/or take time off. Sometimes your short-term goals will take over your long-term goals. Don't worry. There might be a time when what you thought you wanted, with all your heart, fades. That's ok. God has something else for you.

EXPERIENCE YOUR BEAUTY

It may be hard at times to trust that everything will be ok. This is the time for you to reach out to someone you trust, share your fears, anxieties, and worries. There are a lot of wise women in your life who would love to share wisdom, strength, reassurance, and His truth with you. Remember that NO piece of paper, diplomas, job title, social media accounts, nor even success defines you.

God will call you to your purpose in His time, and God will use every bit of your life experiences for His glory. Nothing will be lost, ruined, or for not. Start down your life's road and see where God takes you. Oh, and don't worry, God knows where you're going.

TODAY'S PRAYER

Lord, as I come to a close with this book, nestle inside the core of my heart the ultimate purpose you have for me. Open my eyes to see it; show me the path ahead. Be the lamp onto my footstep. Strengthen me with courage and strength. Lead me. Go before me and behind me. Your love casting out fear. You created me with a purpose. Ignite that vision in me now, and let me boldly step into my dreams ahead, hand-in-hand with you, Amen Jesus, Amen, and Amen.

TAKE ACTION

1. Looking at your life so far, can you see where God has stepped in and changed what you envisioned for your life?

2. What can keep you from fulfilling the purpose that God has for you?

3. How can you prepare for that "such a time as this" moment in your life?

_____

_____

_____

_____

_____

_____

_____

How does it affect the mirror of your heart when you realize that God has made you beautiful for his purpose?

JOURNAL

ABOUT
THE WRITERS

God brought this book together specifically with you in mind. We have had many friends from age 12 to mid-20's read, write and pour their lives into each chapter.

ALEXANDRA SIMM, a college student majoring in History and minoring in Art History and International Studies, worked hard on every story to bring even more relevancy to the message for you. She loves art, writing, and editing. She plans on becoming a lawyer.

NATALIE REYES, a high school student, fearlessly crafted words to connect to you. She plans on going to college for book editing and marketing. In addition, she enjoys being part of her church worship team and reading.

MICHELLE (mom), NATALIE (age 16) and ALEXI (age 13), AGUERREVERE and OLIVIA DEAMICIS (age 17), and EMMA DYER (age 11) read each page and gave feedback for our writers to make changes to help you relate even more. JENNIE (grandma), CARRIE (mom) and ADELE (age 12) CHANDLER contributed, too.

MADELINE KING designed the cover, art, and colorful interior, making it pretty for you.

MICHELLE COX (Co-author of Divine Beauty: Becoming Beautiful based on God's Truth) inspired the format flow of the devotional, while Literally Precise created the layout. We thank you so much!

Morgan Threadgill

is a young Public Relations professional from Austin, Texas. She holds a bachelor's degree in Advertising, Marketing, and Communications from The Fashion Institute of Technology and is a writing enthusiast. All in all, she is a "normal" (what is normal anyways) girl just like you who is passionate about helping others find themselves through Jesus.

Jenn Gotzon

an award-winning actress, plays historical characters in two Oscar-Nominated films, Frost/Nixon and Alone Yet Not Alone. Gotzon trends on Netflix and Prime in faith-based movies like Forgiven, My Daddy Is In Heaven, & The Farmer and The Belle. She enjoys producing inspirational movies, speaking at schools, and making memories with her husband Jim, her son "Baby James" and family. In addition, Gotzon created a jewelry line for QVC and hit billboards as an international model in China. Her passion is to inspire and impact audiences through the art of storytelling on film.

Connect with Jenn on IG @JennGotzon
JennGotzon.com

Dr. Lynnette Simm

didn't let her dyslexia stop her from getting her degrees in psychology and education. She is a writer, speaker, documentary producer, and author. She is the author of And the Day Came, an inspirational, redemptive love story and memoir, and producer of the documentary Tear Stained Forgiveness: Finding Hope and Restoration After Abuse. She has a private practice as a Life Mentor, working with young women and couples. Dr. Simm has been married to Madison for 26 years and they share two daughters.

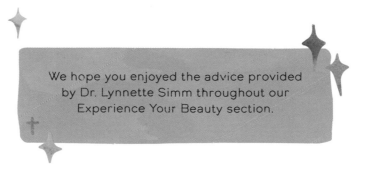

We hope you enjoyed the advice provided by Dr. Lynnette Simm throughout our Experience Your Beauty section.

ABOUT
OUR SPONSOR

Kendall Michelle Daigle was a writer, a beautiful artistic girl, more of the next world than this world, more spirit than body. Kendall influenced so many lives through her compassion, enthusiasm, and artistic talents. Her smile alone could lift anyone's spirits, and her kind actions would go far beyond that. Kendall will continue to impact the world by reaching out far and wide through her words experienced in the book "A Soul Under Construction."

Kendall died 9 days before her 20th birthday. Her words live on. Her memory lives on. Her spirit lives on.

FUNDS ESTABLISHED IN MEMORY OF KENDALL:
- The Kendall Michelle Daigle Memorial Endowment for English at Loyola University New Orleans
- The Kendall Michelle Daigle Fund at the New Orleans Center for Creative Arts (NOCCA)
- The Kendall Michelle Daigle Fund "The Ulster Project" of New Orleans

Our mission invites you to donate to one or all three of our funds by going to the website asoulunderconstruction.com and selecting "donate" to help change the world through Kendall's caring.

Michelle also published a book of Kendall's writings: *A Soul Under Construction*, which will be made into a major motion picture with God's grace. All of the family's earnings from the book and motion picture will be dedicated to Kendall Cares' endowment funds and to help young ladies struggling with drug addiction. The book, A Soul Under Construction can also be ordered from asoulunderconstruction.com.

ABOUT

THE FARMER AND THE BELLE BRAND

Created By:
JENN GOTZON, JIM E. CHANDLER and JOEL BUNKOWSKE

Enjoy our collection of gifts. Discount code: DivineBeauty
TheFarmerandTheBelle.net/shop

Based on biblical and psychological truths, The Farmer and The Belle™ franchise offers emotional security so that people can experience their beauty and genuine love from God. We provide a biblical pathway to transform into the divinely beautiful person you are created to be.

MOVIE: The Farmer and The Belle: Saving Santaland is a funny rom-com made with family at its core. It became a best seller and one of the most watched Christmas movies on Amazon. Inspired by the lead actors, Jenn Gotzon and Jim E. Chandler's true story, they married on their film set.

BRACELET: Our #Beauty Bracelet™ has a beautiful adjustable chain with twenty inscriptions engraved across five coin-size charms affirming what God defines as true beauty. The fifth charm is a heart that falls into the palm of your hand and is designed to grasp when you are feeling insecure or "some kind of way."

NECKLACE: Our heart locket has *Open my Heart* engraved on the outside. When you open the beautiful detachable clasp, *Beauty is on the Inside* is revealed.

ADULT DEVOTIONAL BOOK: Divine Beauty: Becoming Beautiful Based on God's Truth is a 30-Day Devotional book by Michelle Cox and Jenn Gotzon. It will provide a spa for the soul equipping women of all ages to see themselves as God sees them.

CHILDREN'S BOOK: Beautiful Mable written by VeggieTales co-creator Mike Nawrocki with watercolor illustrations by Sara Jo Floyd @Bryantonfarm. The story follows Mable, who does not have the 3 P's. She's not pretty, plump, or productive, but she has a kind heart and teaches the chicks at Hen Haus what beauty is.

SONG: Magnificent Masterpiece, a powerful song written and performed by Beckah Shae, sings the truths around the #Beauty Bracelet™ and the message of the books.

VIDEO BIBLE STUDIES: Adult and Teens follow both books, Divine Beauty and Beauty & Likes, which are led by actress and the book's co-author Jenn Gotzon.

Our #Beauty Bracelet™ is designed by Jenn Cotzon with a beautiful adjustable chain that holds five charms engraved with the chapters from Beauty & Likes. The fifth charm falls into the palm of your hand, allowing you to grasp Jesus' hand in prayer. "Dear Jesus, help me grasp how wide, long, high, and deep is your love for me."

Did you enjoy *Beauty & Likes?* Watch Belle Winters (played by Jenn Gotzon) discover inner beauty as a famous model in Amazon Best-Seller, Award-Winning *The Farmer and The Belle: Saving Santaland* on YouTube, iTunes, Apple TV, Tubi, Amazon FreeVee, and more.